About the Author

Cynthia Mascott was born and raised in Los Angeles. Her ties to Martha's Vineyard Island date back 20 years to when her sister was married there. In 1994, Cynthia moved to the Island and fell in love with its distinct beauty and charm.

For many years, Cynthia has worked as an Assistant Producer for an independent film company based in Hollywood. In the early 1980s she wrote feature articles and music critiques for *Rock* magazine. While living on the Vineyard, she was a freelance writer for *The Martha's Vineyard Times*. She co-authored an Oral History Project and wrote a monthly health column for the paper. Her love for Martha's Vineyard and Cape Cod inspired her to worte this book.

About the Illustrator

$\mathcal{D}$onna M. Blackburn has been interested in drawing and painting for as long as she can remember. Her parents recognized her talent and sent her to attend weekend classes at the Swain School of Design in New Bedford, Mass.

In school, her art classes were given by Mr. Joseph Rapoza, who supplied her with a good basic art education and fostered her love for creative art. In her junior year she was awarded the Jr./Sr. Awards Scholarship to the Boston Museum School of Fine Arts. Upon graduating from high school in 1967, Donna attended the Art Institute of Boston, where she completed a three-year course as an illustration student. She graduated in 1970.

In 1994 Donna received an Honorary BFA from the Art Institute of Boston. Her fine art paintings are currently exhibited at a local gallery and at seasonal art festivals. She also sells her illustrations to paper product and greeting card companies.

She thanks the author of this book for the opportunity to branch out into the field of book illustration.

Donna M. Blackburn and her husband, David, live on Martha's Vineyard.

Acknowledgements

The author would like to thank her nephew, Charlie Nadler, for his computer expertise and sense of humor. She would also like to thank her sister, Holly Mascott Nadler, for luring her to Martha's Vineyard in the first place.

Donna M. Blackburn would like to thank Joseph F. Rapoza, her art teacher, who encouraged her artistic efforts and provided her with a well-rounded art education.

They are both grateful to Kim André, their editor at Hunter Publishing, who offered them splendid guidance and support.

Dedication

This book is dedicated to Trina &
Laurence Mascott, Ada & Richard
Macomder, and David J. Blackburn.

Contents

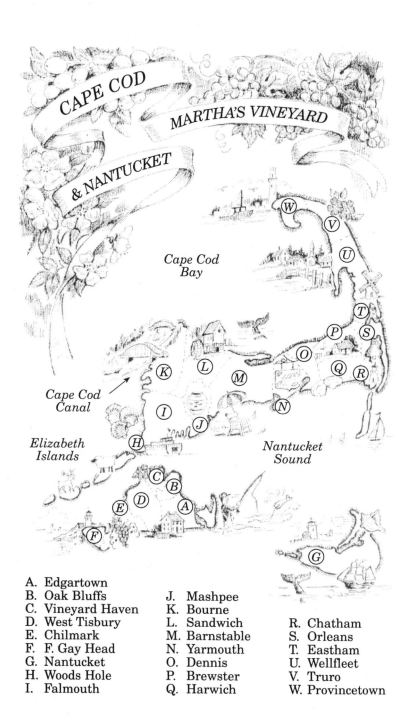

CAPE COD

MARTHA'S VINEYARD

& NANTUCKET

Cape Cod
Bay

Cape Cod
Canal

Elizabeth
Islands

Nantucket
Sound

A. Edgartown
B. Oak Bluffs
C. Vineyard Haven
D. West Tisbury
E. Chilmark
F. F. Gay Head
G. Nantucket
H. Woods Hole
I. Falmouth

J. Mashpee
K. Bourne
L. Sandwich
M. Barnstable
N. Yarmouth
O. Dennis
P. Brewster
Q. Harwich

R. Chatham
S. Orleans
T. Eastham
U. Wellfleet
V. Truro
W. Provincetown

DONNA M. BLACKBURN

Introduction

The breakers looked like droves of a thousand
wild horses of Neptune, rushing to the shore,
with their white manes streaming far behind;
and when, at length the sun shone for a moment,
their manes were rainbow tinted.

~ Henry David Thoreau, Cape Cod, 1817-1862

Looking for an antidote for the doldrums? Take a romantic summer vacation on Cape Cod or the Islands of Martha's Vineyard and Nantucket. Imagine windswept beaches, sailboats and ferries, Victorian houses, and colorful gardens.

Say the names like a mantra: Martha's Vineyard, Nantucket, Cape Cod. Already you are there.

Just a one-hour drive from Boston, Cape Cod offers the sojourner the vacation of a lifetime. The remote beauty of Martha's Vineyard and Nantucket Islands can be reached by plane or ferry.

For the romantic, this book will give you all the requisite information for planning a perfect vacation. Learn more about the hotels, bed and breakfasts and restaurants in the area. We'll give you plenty of suggestions for spending your days, whether you choose to go shopping or want to explore the nearby beaches and forests. And there's nightlife too. You'll have a choice of concerts, plays and nighttime sailing excursions.

So, take a minute and dream.

A Brief History

It was the Wampanoag Indians who first called Cape Cod and the Islands home. They fished the sea, farmed the land, and hunted the forests. The Wampanoags were a peaceful people, living harmoniously among one another. The arrival of European explorers occurred in the 1600s. There are several reports of earlier sojourners, but Bartholomew Gosnold is credited for being the first European to lay claim to Cape Cod. Arriving in 1602, Gosnold named the area after the plentiful cod he and his ship crew found in the waters.

Eighteen years later, passengers aboard the *Mayflower* spent a month on the Cape, near Provincetown, before resettling in nearby Plymouth. Once the Pilgrims became adjusted to their life in Plymouth, they began to spread out southward, with several different groups moving to the Cape. The towns of Sandwich, Barnstable, Yarmouth and Eastham were the first areas to be settled. The Indian and white settlers lived side by side, in peaceful co-existence during those early years.

The Cape and Islands were horribly exposed to English attack during the Revolutionary War. There was little that the Cape Codders and Islanders could do to keep away the British forces. Yet each town has recorded separate acts of heroism, from the three Vineyard girls who blew up a flagpole rather than allow the British to beat them to the task, to the Cape Cod and Island men who lost their lives while fighting for freedom in America.

They called it the Golden Age of Whaling, and it ran from the late 1700s to the mid-1900s. While the Cape and Island ports offered little protection during a war, the same ports offered wonderful access to the sea. Throughout the 1800s, sea captains traveled the oceans in search of the almighty whale.

The whalers called the Cape and Island their home, but for the most part they lived upon the great ships, often for years at a time. Their wives and children waited for them at home, never knowing when or if they would see their loved ones again. But there were riches to find out at sea, and the captains would arrive home with pockets full of money. They built lavish homes with money they made from whaling, each home grander than its neighbor.

The Golden Age of Whaling came to its eventual conclusion when other sources of fuel became more readily accessible. The Cape and Islands did not see another Golden era until the area was discovered by vacationers, seeking solace from their city lives.

Tourism continues to be a primary business in the area. With it have come some of the negative side-effects found along much of America's popular East Coast. Fortunately, Martha's Vineyard and Nantucket recognized early on the need for restrictive building codes and laws in order to protect the area from overdevelopment. The Cape followed suit, and in 1961 the Cape Cod National Seashore was established to protect the eastern shore line. In 1990, the Cape Commission was organized to overlook further development of the area.

But parts of the Cape have been spoiled. Nowadays, it takes longer to find the pristine beauty of the Cape than it used to, but it is still there. This guide will give you many tips on out-of-the-way romantic beaches, coves, forests and preserves. It will give you intimate accounts of the many wonderful lodging opportunities available, from reconstructed farmhouses to renovated stately sea captain homes and more. All you'll need to bring is this book and your heart.

The Land & Sea

The Cape Cod peninsula is situated about 50 miles southeast of Boston. Entry to the Cape is via the Sagamore and Bourne bridges. Take note of the majestic span of the bridges with the Cape Canal below. The 17.4-mile Cape Cod Canal is 480 feet wide and is the world's widest sea-level canal.

As you travel over the bridge, you have officially arrived on the Cape. The **Upper Cape** is comprised of Falmouth, Woods Hole, Bourne, Mashpee, and Sandwich. This region of the Cape is relatively unspoiled. It faces Buzzards Bay to the west, and the

Vineyard Sound to the south. The **Mid-Cape** towns of Barnstable, Hyannis, Yarmouth, and Dennis are more heavily populated. Hyannis is the largest town in the area.

D. M. BLACKBURN

As you go farther east, you will reach the **Outer Cape,** comprised of Brewster, Harwich, Chatham, Wellfleet, Orleans, and Truro. At the very tip of the Cape is Provincetown, often referred to as the **Outer Cape.** The southern shore of the Cape (from Woods Hole to Chatham) faces the Vineyard and Nantucket sounds. Warmed by the Gulf Stream, the Sound has mild surf and warmer waters. The eastern shores of the Cape face the Atlantic Ocean. While the beaches along the Atlantic are wide and sandy, the waters are generally cooler there, and the surf more vigorous.

❦

An Indian Legend

An Indian legend told repeatedly in history books about Nantucket and Martha's Vineyard Island talks of an Indian God and legendary whaleman, Moshup. Lost at sea, he smoked a pipe as he contemplated his situation. The ashes from his pipe became the Islands; the smoke became the fog.

❦

In actuality, the Islands and the Cape were formed by a retreating glacier in the last Ice Age. The region offers a natural habitat for many birds and sea creatures, from seabirds to waterfowl and from whales to starfish and sea urchins. In the Cape's forests you will find pine trees, marshes, cranberry bogs and a variety of other plants and flowers indigenous to the area. The coastal terrain varies from the noble Gay Head Cliffs to the Atlantic's windswept sand dunes. The shore is ever-changing in all of its glory.

Climate

The Cape and Islands have a relatively mild coastal climate. A general rule of thumb is that the region will be about 10° cooler than Boston throughout the summer. In the winter, while the winds may rage and the land can be covered by snow, the coastal air keeps the area warmer than inland.

In winter months, expect the temperature to drop into the mid-20s; it usually gets no higher than the mid-40s. During spring, sunny, crisp days are the norm, with highs in the mid-50s and lows in the mid-40s. Average summer temperatures are a comfortable 60-70°. Fall sees warm days of anywhere from 40-60°, while cooler days can drop into the mid-20s.

Now that you have reviewed the year's temperatures, forget any standards which have been written here. The climate is changeable on the Cape and its islands. A nice day may suddenly bring a storm. A torrential rain may clear to bright skies. Bring a bathing suit and a rain jacket in the summer (you'll need both).

Government & Economy

Several industries thrive on the Cape and the Islands. The tourist industry has long been associated with the area, from the hotels and restaurants to the car, bicycle and boat rentals, clothing and antique shops and more. Tourism provides jobs for many locals, fuels the economy and guarantees visitors a happy holiday.

There are plenty of lobsters, scallops, freshwater and saltwater fish still in the waters off the Cape and Islands, and fishing continues to be a thriving industry. At any of the local ports you will find fishermen coming in and out of the harbors, their nets full of the sea's treasures.

While the amount of agricultural land in the area has diminished, there are still many working farms. And there is something quite wonderful about passing by them. Horses, sheep and cows craze the pastures and the fertile fields yield corn, tomatoes and other vegetables. Roadside stands sell fresh fruits, vegetables and flowers. You have traveled back in time.

Many professionals with families have chosen to move to the Cape and the Islands to raise their children in the safe environment the region offers. Some choose to commute daily to Boston, others have had the good fortune to find work where they live.

The Cape and the Islands have long been a haven for writers, artists and other creative sorts. Henry David Thoreau wrote *Cape Cod* over a hundred years ago. The book chronicles his trip through the Lower Cape. Martha's Vineyard Island is the home of many celebrities: Mike Wallace, Art Buchwald, Carly Simon, James Taylor, and Ted Danson, to name a few.

Choosing to be part of the local community, many of the celebrities have taken part in the local fundraising events, with proceeds going toward local charities and institutions. Nantucket has recently begun an Annual Film Festival and Provincetown continues to be a recognized artist community.

People & Culture

Perhaps the most pronounced personality trait among the people who live here is the hearty individualism that seems to be part and parcel of every resident. Another quality indigenous to the area is a sense of cooperation and the acceptance of others, regardless of differences. It's a place where faces are familiar and everyone knows your name.

The Wampanoag Tribe were the first inhabitants of the area, and although their numbers have diminished, their Native American influence is part of the local culture. People who have lived on the Cape and Islands for centuries will proudly tell you how many generations their people have called the area home. There are strong Portuguese and Cape Verde communities throughout Southwestern Massachusetts. African-Americans found Oak Bluffs to be the perfect summer resort and have vacationed there since the late 1900s. A strong gay community in Provincetown has thrived over the years.

There's a definite distinction between native-born people and those born elsewhere: You're ahead of the game and given a higher social status if you were born here. Even if you moved here in your first year of life, you are not considered a native by those who were born here. But not to worry, you will be accepted over a period of time. Ultimately, the people of the Cape and Islands are a hearty bunch of individuals who will stop and say hello, help you when you need assistance, and will always express their loyalty to their home.

Price Chart

For Inns & Hotels

$$$$ . . . . $200+ per night

$$$ . . . . $100-$200 per night

$$ . . . . less than $100 per night

For Restaurants

$$$$ . . . . $30+ per person

$$$ . . . . $20-$30 per person

$$ . . . . $10-$20 per person

$ . . . . below $10 per person

Throughout this book you will see certain hotels and inns highlighted with a cherub. These are the author's personal choices of the most romantic places to stay.

Martha's Vineyard Island

Only seven miles separate Martha's Vineyard from the mainland, yet in many ways the Island seems worlds apart from the frenetic tempo of modern life. The Island attracts the rich and famous, but it also offers all travelers a chance to vacation in isolated beauty.

It's an island of forests, rolling hills, sand and water. During the day, the sun glistens on the Atlantic Ocean, and at night the moon blazes a path over the water. Seagrass sways in the breeze, waves lap the sand, and seaswept driftwood haphazardly decorates the beach. Children swim in the water or search for sea glass. Sailboats drift out toward the horizon.

Even away from the beach, you're never far from water. The many ponds sparkle in the sunlight. The Island's forests and farm lands are stunning. Watch the cows graze in the field, the osprey and geese alighting in their nests.

Six separate towns comprise the Martha's Vineyard Island, each with its own personality and flavor. The three "Down-Island" towns are Edgartown, Oak Bluffs, and Vineyard Haven. "Up-Island" towns include West Tisbury, Chilmark, Menemsha, and Gay Head.

The Down Island towns offer a variety of delights. Edgartown, perhaps the most elegant of them all, is defined by brick sidewalks, narrow streets, stately Colonial and Federal houses, and carefully maintained gardens . The downtown area offers an array of boutiques, gift stores, eateries, and specialty shops.

Travel to Oak Bluffs for its fun-loving atmosphere. Be sure to take a ride on the Flying Horses, one of the nation's oldest carousels. The Methodist Camp Grounds, just steps away from the downtown area, is the crowning jewel of Oak Bluffs. You'll enter a fairytale land of tiny gingerbread houses painted all colors of the rainbow.

Vineyard Haven is the Island's commercial center. A stroll down Main Street brings you to first-rate boutiques and antique shops, as well as an array of restaurants, pizza establishments and ice cream shops. Spectacular vistas of land and sea will take your breath away as you travel up-island. If you're looking for the flavor of an old New England village, you'll want to visit the towns of West Tisbury, Chilmark, and Gay Head.

Many, many people travel from all parts of the world to the Island. The Vineyard has a magical call, and if you hear it, you will return again and again.

History

$\mathcal{T}$he history of the Island is colorful and varied. The first inhabitants were members of the Wampanoag Indian tribe, whose economy was based on farming and fishing. The earliest written report of the Vineyard was made in 1602 by the Reverend John Breretorn and Gabriel Archer, who sailed aboard Captain Bartholomew Gosnold's ship.

In 1641, Thomas Mayhew of Watertown, Massachusetts purchased the Vineyard, Nantucket and the Elizabeth Islands for £40 from two English noblemen who held Royal land grants to the area. Mayhew's son, Thomas Mayhew, Jr., arrived with a group a year later and settled in the Edgartown area, initially named Great Harbor. In 1671, the town was renamed Edgartown in honor of the infant son of the Duke of York.

The White settlers and Indians co-existed peacefully during the Colonial period. However, as the settlers began to build Edgartown, the Indians eventually moved out to Chappaquiddick and Gay Head.

During the Revolutionary War, English troops attacked the Vineyard. On September 10, 1778, 82 ships and 10,000 British soldiers raided the Island, primarily stealing livestock and burning many ships in the harbor. The Islanders knew they were outnumbered and did not fight back, but nonetheless they were angered by the attack.

Edgartown and Vineyard Haven became principal ports by the turn of the 19th century. Whaling was Edgartown's chief industry in the early 1820s. Island men (and a handful of women) traveled the seas of the world in pursuit of the almighty whale. Many of the stately captain's homes were built during that time.

The Whaling Era (from the late 1800s to the mid-1900s, came to an end during the Civil War when many of the Island's ships were captured by the Confederate navy. As newer fuel products were introduced the whaling industry declined. The Vineyard began attracting summer visitors during the late 19th century. The Island's first summer resort was established in the Oak Bluffs Methodist Camp Grounds. At first, the campground was used for religious revivals, with visitors staying in makeshift tents. As it gained in popularity, the colorful cottages were built and the beginning of the tourist industry was born.

The beauty of the Island, its peacefulness and unique charm, continues to beckon travelers to its shores over a century later.

DONNA M. BLACKBURN

Martha's Vineyard

Edgartown

Traveling to Edgartown is like time travel. You'll think you are living again in the early 19th century. Gas lamps illuminate the downtown streets. Stately Federal-style sea captains' homes grace the neighborhoods. Carefully tended gardens create splashes of color. Cinematic views of Nantucket Sound and Chappaquiddick Island are around each corner.

The people of Edgartown are proud of their community and have made every effort to preserve its history. Many of the buildings are registered with the Martha's Vineyard Preservation Trust. Most of the inns and hotels have colorful histories, and have been fully restored to their original splendor.

Nearby beaches and forest preserves offer romantic sweeping views and tranquil resting places. As the day ends, enjoy a romantic dinner at any of the picturesque restaurants in town. Go to a movie or concert, or sit at the Memorial Wharf and watch the sunset.

Welcome Romantic Inns & Hotels

The Harborview Inn

Overlooking Edgartown Harbor, the Harborview Inn is one of the oldest hotels in the region. Built in 1891, the hotel has been carefully restored to its original splendor. You won't find a better view anywhere on the Island than from one of the waterfront suites and guest rooms. All waterfront rooms feature queen- or king-size beds. A newer addition in the rear offers guest rooms, suites and one- and two-bedroom cottages. Sip a cup of tea or an evening cocktail as you enjoy the view from the verandah while sitting in an old-fashioned rocking chair. There's a large outdoor pool, private beach and tennis courts for hotel guests. The rooms are climate-controlled, and the hotel offers room service, telephone, hairdryer, iron and ironing board, color television and cable, and AM/FM radio. Concierge service and private parking are available. Open all year.

The Harborview Hotel
131 N. Water Street
Box 7
Edgartown, MA 02539
Reservations, ☎ 800-225-6005
Fax 508-627-7845
Hotel, ☎ 508-627-7000
$$$$

The Kelley House

This 59-room country inn has a Colonial charm about it. Dating back 250 years, the main building was an 18th-century inn. Enjoy the two-story lobby with its intimate lure of bygone years. Ocean- and garden-view suites and rooms are available for our romantics.

In keeping with its sense of history, the rooms offer authentic period furniture and colorful quilts. Each room has a telephone, television and air-conditioning. A complimentary continental breakfast is served each day.

The Kelley House is located in downtown Edgartown; you can't beat the location. Enjoy the Kelley House pub, called the Newes from America. It's an Island favorite, offering casual dining amid a vintage pub setting. Open from May to October.

The Kelley House
23 Kelley Street
P.O. Box 7
Edgartown, MA 02539
Reservations, ☎ 800-225-6005
Fax 508-627-7845
Hotel, ☎ 508-627-7900
$$$$

Martha's Vineyard

The Victorian Inn

The Victorian Inn was built in 1820 during the heyday of Edgartown's whaling period. The hotel is listed in the National Register of Historic Places. Located near downtown, many rooms have views of the harbor. Simple elegance and quaint decor define the hotel. The inn has been carefully restored and the owners promise a relaxing, hospitable, and comfortable stay. A complimentary gourmet breakfast is served daily in the breakfast room, or in the inn's lovely English garden (weather permitting). Open throughout the year.

The Victorian Inn
24 South Water Street
Edgartown, MA 02539
☎ 508-627-4784
www.thevic.com
$$$

The Edgartown Inn

If you have ever entertained the fantasy of staying in the same room as someone who was rich or famous, then a stay at The Edgartown Inn might meet your requirements. The inn has a list of illustrious guests from Daniel Webster and Nathaniel Hawthorne to John F. Kennedy.

Nathaniel Hawthorne conducted a romance with Edgartown resident Eliza Gibbs for over a year while he stayed at the inn.

The Edgartown Inn was built in 1798 as a residence for a Captain Thomas Worth. His son, William Jenkins Worth, was a hero in the Mexican War. In fact, Fort Worth, Texas, was named after him.

The 12 rooms in the main house are furnished with antiques and have a distinctive Victorian flair. Outside of each room are brass plaques presented by the Daughters of the American Revolution, listing the names of former distinguished guests. The Garden House, in the back of the inn, offers several more rooms with private balconies overlooking the garden. The Barn has also been restored and includes two rooms with private baths and three rooms with shared baths.

A country breakfast is served daily in the patio garden and in the cozy breakfast room. Open year-round.

The Edgartown Inn
56 N. Water Street
Box 1211
Edgartown, MA 02539
☎ *508-627-4794*
$$$

✈ The Shiverick Inn

Beautiful and elegant, the Shiverick Inn offers its guests a romantic and glamorous place to stay. Eighteenth- and 19th-century English and American antiques and furnishings give the inn its historical flavor.

DONNA M. BLACKBURN

The inn was built in 1840 for the town physician, Dr. Clement Francis Shiverick, and reflects the Greek Revival period. As you enter, double doors with frosted etched glass open up to a sweeping staircase.

The owners of the Shiverick boast that the rooms are one-of-a-kind and the "guest rooms, suites and common rooms recall a bygone era that transports visitors back to a time when dedication to tradition, elegance, and comfort were imperative."

Enjoy a complimentary breakfast in the breakfast room with its black rought iron tables and chairs.

Located at the corner of Pease Point Way and Pent Lane, the Shiverick is a short distance from Edgartown's downtown. Open all year.

> *The Shiverick Inn*
> *P.O. Box 640*
> *Edgartown, MA 02539*
> ☎ *508-627-3797*
> *Fax 508-627-8441*
> ☎ *800-723-4292*
> *$$$$*

✈ The Charlotte Inn

One of the most elegant inns in Edgartown, the Charlotte Inn, located just outside Edgartown's downtown area, is a tribute to Edwardian England. Colorful gardens, a plush interior and loving care are the hallmark here.

Each room is beautifully decorated with careful attention to detail. Sleep like royalty in an ornate four-poster cherrywood canopy bed, complete with goose-down pillows and comforters. Or nestle by the fireplace as you read from one of the leather-bound books on the shelves.

The main building dates from 1864. Take some time to view the artwork, from the present work of local artists such as Ray Ellis to the 19th-century oil paintings. The Green Room offers breakfast in the morning and tea or a drink in the afternoon and evening. The room features burnished mahogany paneling, a roaring fire, and deep hunter green decor. The Carriage House has several rooms with private terraces, fireplaces,

DONNA M. BLACKBURN

French doors and brick courtyards. The romantic Coach House suite offers complete privacy, cathedral ceilings, a view of the harbor, and lovely furnishings. Open throughout the year.

The Charlotte Inn
27 South Summer Street
Edgartown, MA 02539
☎ *508-627-4751*
Fax 508-627-4652
$$$$

✈ The Tuscany Inn

Light and airy, cheerful and romantic, the Tuscany Inn has a European flavor in a Victorian setting. Formerly the Captain Fisher House, the Tuscany Inn was recently renovated by Laura Sbrana and Rusty Scheuer. Laura (an interior decorator and gourmet cook) can be credited for the inn's excellent interior design and for the gourmet dishes served in the restaurant, La Cucina. Laura is a native of Tuscany, and the Italian influence can be seen throughout the inn. This is one of the most charming places to stay in the Edgartown area.

DONNA M. BLACKBURN

Toile print wallpaper and matching furnishings provide a sense of whimsy throughout. Gingham and floral prints in the indoor dining room and living room gives a European flavor.

La Boheme suite, replete with an Edgartown Harbor view and a private whirlpool under a skylight, couldn't be more romantic.

Dine in the lovely indoor dining area, amid brightly colored gingham tablecloths and Italian baskets and treasures. Or, on sunny days, sit in the outdoor La Cucina Ristorante. A full gourmet breakfast is served daily and is part of the room rate.

Ask about the inn's cooking school, where you can learn the secrets for cooking the perfect Italian cuisine from owner Laura Sbrana. A Cooking School Weekend package is offered throughout the spring and fall only, but the inn is open year-round.

The Tuscany Inn
22 N. Water Street
Box 2428
Edgartown, MA 02539
☎ *508-627-5999/8999/6605*
$$$$

The Daggett House

Three centuries of architecture are featured at the Daggett House. The tavern originates from 1660. A century later the Daggett House was built. It has seven guest rooms and two suites, several with views of the Edgartown Harbor. The Daggett also offers rooms across the street its Captain Warren House, an excellent example of a 19th-century Greek revival captain's home. The most romantic option at the Captain Warren House is the penthouse suite. Climb the iron staircase to the widow's walk. Sit in the roof top hot tub and relax, enjoying views of the harbor.

The Dagget House maintains its history and authenticity, with furnishings and paintings representative of Edgartown's whaling past. Open all year.

The Daggett House
59 N. Water Street
Edgartown, MA 02539
☎ *508-627-4600*
Fax 508-627-4611
☎ *800-946-3400*
www.welcomeinn.com/daggett
$$$

Captain Dexter's House of Edgartown

The ambience of the Captain Dexter House is one of warmth and friendliness. The house dates back to 1840. Antique furnishings, hand-sewn quilts, and period reproduction wallpaper give the rooms an inviting air. Many of the rooms have fireplaces.

A complimentary continental breakfast is offered. Visit with the other guests in the dining room or sit outside in one of the flower gardens.

Captain Dexter House of Edgartown
Box 279835
Pease Point Way
Edgartown, MA 02539
☎ 508-627-7289
$$$

Restaurants

Starbucks

Located at the Harborview Inn, Starbucks offers a full breakfast, lunch and dinner menu. The spacious dining room overlooks the harbor. Dinner choices include lobster soufflé, pan-seared breast of duck and other seafood and meat specialties. Starbucks also serves a bountiful Sunday brunch. Reservations are recommended.

Starbucks
131 North Water Street
Edgartown, MA 02539
☎ 508-627-7000
$$$$

L'etoile

Revel in the wonders of nouvelle French cuisine at one of Edgartown's most elegant restaurants. Situated in the Charlotte Inn, L'etoile offers an intimate dinner set in a beautiful conservatory restaurant. Choose from such entrées as curry roasted halibut or étouffée of native lobster. The restaurant serves lunch and dinner during the summer season. Reservations are recommended.

> *L'etoile*
> *27 South Summer Street*
> ☎ *508-627-5187*
> *$$$$*

O'Briens Serious Seafood and Grill

Dine in elegance in O'Briens indoor restaurant or amid twinkling lights in the garden. Gourmet recipes enhance local seafood, meats and produce. Entrées include such delicacies as blackened swordfish medallions, mussels over linguine with a garlic butter sauce, or grilled Long Island duck breast. Reservations are recommended.

> *O'Briens*
> *137 Upper Main Street*
> ☎ *508-627-5850*
> *$$$$*

The Daggett House Restaurant

Dine overlooking the harbor at the historical Daggett House. The ancient beehive fireplace dates back to the late 1600s. Ask about the secret staircase leading up to a guest room on the next floor. The restaurant offers New England country breakfasts and dinners. Reservations are recommended.

> *The Daggett House*
> *59 North Water Street*
> ☎ *508-627-4600*
> *$$$*

La Cucina Ristorante

The Northern Italian cuisine at La Cucina Ristorante can't be beat. Located at the Tuscany Inn, the restaurant's garden setting creates a romantic mood for lovers. As you dine by candlelight, choose from such entrées as rosemary- and lavender-marinated lamb chops or lobster risotto. Reservations are recommended.

La Cucina Ristorante
22 N. Water Street
☎ 508-627-8161
$$$$

Lattanzi's

Enjoy traditional Italian cuisine, wood-grilled specialties, handmade pasta and fresh seafood and lobster dishes. Choose from hickory grilled veal porterhouse chop with porcini mushroom cream, grilled filet of beef with prosciutto and other enjoyable feasts. Reservations are recommended.

Lattanzi's
Old Post Office Square
☎ 508-627-8854
$$$

Savoir Fare

Savoir Fare's intimate patio setting lends itself to romance. The restaurant serves lunch and dinner. Dinner specialties include soft-shell crabs over creamy lemon risotto, grilled marinated semi-boneless quail with mascarpone tortellini and other gourmet delights. Enjoy the breezy patio seating as you sit amid twinkling lights.

Savoir Fare
Post Office Square
☎ 508-627-9864
$$$

The Shiretown Inn

The restaurant's covered terrace garden setting behind the Shiretown Inn is particularly romantic. Dinner choices include dry-aged filet mignon with grilled portabello mushrooms, herb-crusted rack of lamb with rosemary and fresh mint, and other seafood and meat dishes. Reservations are recommended.

> *The Shiretown Inn*
> *N. Water Street*
> ☎ *508-627-6655*
> *$$$$*

The Navigator Restaurant

Enjoy a casual dining experience with a superb waterfront view of the harbor. New England seafood specialties are served at reasonable prices.

> *The Navigator Restaurant*
> *2 Main Street*
> ☎ *508-627-4320*
> *$$$*

The Seafood Shanty

The Seafood Shanty, also with views of the harbor, offers an assortment of fresh seafoods and provides musical entertainment throughout the summer.

> *Seafood Shanty*
> *31 Dock Street*
> ☎ *508-627-8622*
> *$$$*

Other Eateries

The **Black Dog Restaurant and General Stores** have opened a new shop in Edgartown. Located on Summer Street (near the Charlotte Inn), savor the famous Black Dog coffees, breads, baked goods and other take-out foods. The store also has a full array of Black Dog catalogue items, including T-shirts, sweatshirts and hats. *Summer Street,* ☎ *508-627-3360.*

Also a Vineyard favorite is **Mad Martha's Homemade Ice Cream**. Choose from a vast array of ice creams, yogurts, and other sweet offerings at Edgartown's Mad Martha's. *7 N. Water Street,* ☎ *508-627-8761.*

The **Old Stone Bakery** has the freshest, most delicious doughnuts, apple fritters, cheese breads and other baked items. A favorite of mine and many other Vineyarders. *N. Water Street,* ☎ *508-627-5880.*

Gourmet Shops

Planning a romantic lunch? Consider shopping at one of Edgartown's gourmet shops where you'll find a wonderful selection of scrumptious lunch items. They'll pack a picnic basket for you, including wines.

Soigne, *190 Upper Main Street, Edgartown, MA 02539,* ☎ *508-627-8489. $*

Seasoned To Taste, *3 Nevin Square,* ☎ *508-627-7800. $*

Great Harbor Gourmet Spirits, *40 Main Street,* ☎ *508-627-4390. $*

Truly Scrumptious Caterers, *11 S. Summer Street,* ☎ *508-627-3990. $*

Touring Edgartown

The best way to see Edgartown is on foot. Stroll past the famous homes and buildings that make Edgartown unique.

The **Martha's Vineyard Preservation Trust** (☎ 508-627-8017 or 627-4441, owns and operates the Vincent House Museum, the Old Whaling Church and the Dr. Daniel Fisher House.

The **Dr. Daniel Fisher House**, 99 Main Street, was built in 1840 and is an excellent example of Federal-style architecture. Open to the public through the Edgartown Historical Walking Tours (☎ 508-627-8619) the house was beautifully redecorated in 1992. It may be rented for weddings, parties, receptions and other special events. ☎ 508-627-4440.

Behind the Fisher House is one of the oldest homes on the Island, **The Vincent House** (circa 1675). The Vincent House Museum, off Pease Point Way, offers its visitors a chance to see a structure built over 300 years ago. It has much of its original brickwork, hardware, and woodwork. ☎ 508-627-8017.

The **Old Whaling Church**, 89 Main Street, was built in 1843. With its dramatic front columns and majestic steeple, it's an excellent example of Greek Revival architecture. The church is now a community performing arts center and has many special events scheduled throughout the year. Lectures, films, concerts, plays, and other community activities take place at the Whaling Church. Call the church or consult the local papers for a schedule of events. ☎ 508-627-4442.

Take note of the **Dukes County Court House** at 70 Main Street. It was built in 1858 and was one of the first brick buildings erected on the Island. Take a stroll down North Water Street, lined by picture-perfect stately houses. The 19th-century homes were built during Edgartown's whaling days. You'll see many a widow's walk atop the homes, aptly named for the women who would look searchingly toward the sea for their husbands return from their distant adventures. Notice the mannequin of a woman on the widow's walk at The Captain's House, located on North Water Street.

One of the most beautiful sights is the **Edgartown Lighthouse** at the end of North Water Street. It is particularly splendid at night, when the twin beams from the lighthouse and the moon shine over the harbor. Years ago, a wooden walk – called "The Bridge of Sighs" – led to the lighthouse. It was the place where the young men and women romanced one another, before saying good-bye as the men went off to sea.

Walk past the Harborview Hotel on Starbuck Neck. When it dead-ends at Fuller Street, take a left and head back toward downtown. The second house on the right, past the tennis courts, is the **Emily Post House**. Famous for her words of wisdom regarding etiquette, Ms. Post was a summer resident of Edgartown.

To the west of downtown is **The Vineyard Museum and Dukes County Historical Society**, at the intersection of School and Cooke Street. Several buildings comprise the museum and it is considered one of the best in the region. ☎ 508-627-4441. The **Thomas Cooke House**, on the museum property, was built in 1765 and is an excellent example of pre-Revolutionary War architecture. The 12 rooms include whaling artifacts, antique furniture, and the costumes and gear used by the sea men and early farmers. Also on the museum grounds is the world-famous two-story **Fresnel lens**, installed in the Gay Head Lighthouse in 1856. The main building of the museum is the **Francis Foster Museum** and the **Gale Huntington Library of History**. Next door is the **Captain Francis Pease House**, where you will find an art gallery, displays of Indian artifacts and other exhibits. ☎ 508-627-4441.

Take note of the **First Federated Church**, located next to the museum. Built in 1828 as a Congregation Church, it merged with the Baptist Church in the early 1900s to become the Federated Church. It has maintained its original beauty, including the original wooden box pews.

Resume your walk down Cooke Street and make a left at **South Water Street**. The homes on this street were built during Edgartown's whaling days and are superb examples of the architecture of those times. As you pass Davis Lane, take a look at the **Pagoda Tree**. It was brought back from China in a flower pot and now stands tall in front of the Harborside Inn.

After you arrive back in the downtown section of Edgartown, walk toward the harbor and rest at **The Memorial Wharf**. The wharf offers lovely vistas of the harbor and Chappaquiddick Island.

Just a stone's throw away from Edgartown is **Chappaquiddick**. which offers the romantic visitors a chance to enjoy the beauty of its parks and Atlantic-facing beaches. You'll need to take the Chappaquiddick ferry to reach these spots. The ferry is a delight. Crossing the Edgartown harbor takes about two minutes. There is no specific sailing schedule, but runs are made regularly through the day and evening. The ferries are called *On Time I, II,* and *III*. You might have a wait if you plan to travel to Chappaquiddick by car (the ferry offers only two or three spaces for cars) so consider renting a bicycle or walking.

DONNA M. BLACKBURN

Walking Tours

To learn more about the traditions and history of Edgartown, take a **Edgartown Historical Walking Tour**, sponsored by the Martha's Vineyard Preservation Trust. Call ☎ 508-627-8619 for more information.

Are you aware that Edgartown has many, many ghosts? Don't worry, they're friendly. Holly Nadler, local celebrity, writer and author of the book, *Haunted Island, True Ghost Stories From*

Martha's Vineyard, will take you on a private tour of Edgartown. Call Holly Tours at ☎ 508-693-9321.

 *Outdoor Fun*

Beaches

Katama Beach: On the south shore of Edgartown, at the end of Katama Road, three miles of beach offer surf on one side and a protected salt pond on the other. A shuttle bus will take you there from the center of town ($1.50 one way). If you prefer to drive or bicycle to the beach, follow Pease Point Way three miles from Edgartown.

The **Joseph A. Sylvia State Beach**, which offers two miles of open coast, lies between Edgartown and Oak Bluffs on State Road.

Just a a short distance from downtown, **Lighthouse Beach** offers pleasant swimming conditions and a view of the harbor and lighthouse. Take North Water Street to Starbuck's Neck.

Just across the harbor from Edgartown is **Chappy Point Beach**, with 705 feet of sand and splendid views of the harbor. Take the Chappaquiddick ferry to gain access to the beach.

Forests, Parks & Preserves

Felix Neck Wildlife Sanctuary is a beautiful 350-acre wildlife preserve run by the Massachusetts Audubon Society. Walk through beach marsh lands, open fields and trees along six miles of marked nature trails. Travel toward Vineyard Haven on the Edgartown-Vineyard Haven Road and watch for the sign.

Bask in isolated beauty at the **Caroline Tuthill Preserve**. Walk through barren pines, old cranberry bogs, salt marshes and coastal swamps. From the Edgartown Triangle, travel .4 miles on the Edgartown-Vineyard Haven Road.

You'll find a lovely view of Eel Pond and Nantucket Sound in the 16-acre **Sheriff's Meadow Preserve**. Foot trails lead you through forests and marsh lands. The Sheriff's Meadow is located off Planting Field Way.

Follow Meetinghouse Way to **Meshacket Neck**, a 75-acre preserve owned by the town of Edgartown. Trails lead to Edgartown Great Pond.

Cape Pogue Wildlife Refuge and Wasque Reservation is located on the east side of Chappaquiddick. Take the ferry and follow the main road. The area contains two beaches managed by the Trustees of Reservations. The 509 acres of land are a refuge and breeding habitat for endangered shorebirds. Swimming and fishing are available. An entry fee is charged for non-members of the Trustees of Reservation.

Take the Chappaquiddick ferry and follow the main road for several miles to reach the **My Toi Japanese Gardens** on the left. Enjoy the tranquility of the 14-acre park with brooks, ponds and paths. Owned by the Trustees of Reservations.

Oak Bluffs

𝔉unky is the definitive word to describe Oak Bluffs. Be ready to get down and party with the rest of the folks visiting here. It's a town where you'll go just a little bit mad. Yet, like Alice in *Alice in Wonderland*, you'll be thrilled to be part of the fun and curious to see what will happen next.

The first white settler in Oak Bluffs was John Daggett. He purchased 500 acres of land, naming the area Squash Meadow. It was the influence of the Methodist Revival movement in the early 1800s, however, which put Oak Bluffs on the map. By

1835, Oak Bluffs became a mecca for Methodists seeking spiritual salvation.

In the later part of the 19th century, Oak Bluffs began to capture the imagination of a different crowd, giving birth to the Island's tourist industry. Oak Bluffs became a seaside resort, complete with dancing halls, large hotels, a boardwalk and a roller skating rink. Many of the original buildings were destroyed by fire or replaced over the years, but the spirit of fun is still very much alive.

Today, Oak Bluffs continues to be the center of activity on the Island. It is crowded, a little bit crazy and definitely the town to visit if you're looking for evening entertainment.

DONNA M. BLACKBURN

Welcome

Romantic Inns & Hotels

☘ The Oak House

The Oak House is one of the nicest B&Bs on the Island. It is family operated and lovingly decorated. Enjoy the ocean view from the spacious veranda or from one of the nicely decorated guest rooms. Among your choice of accommodations is the President Ulysses S. Grant Room, a two-room suite decorated in pastel colors with its own balcony overlooking the sea. Or consider one of the beautiful oak panelled rooms, also with views of the ocean.

DONNA M. BLACKBURN

The house was built in 1872 and was at one time owned by the governor of Massachusetts, Governor William Claflin. Every room has its own private bath and telephone and is air-conditioned. Enjoy home cooking at its best. The Oak House offers a complimentary continental breakfast and an afternoon Victorian Tea.

The Oak House
Seaview Avenue, P.O. Box 299
Oak Bluffs, MA 02557
☎ *508-693-4187; fax 508-696-7385*
$$$

The Beach House

The Beach House has a nice friendly feel to it. Located across from the Oak Bluffs Beach, many of the rooms have lovely views of the ocean. There's a wonderful porch, perfect for watching the sunset. Choose from any of the nine guest rooms, each with private baths. A complimentary breakfast buffet is served daily.

The Beach House
P.O. Box 417
Oak Bluffs, MA 02557
☎ *508-693-3955*
$$$

The Admiral Benbow Inn

This charming, turn-of-the-century inn is situated about a half-mile outside of downtown Oak Bluffs. It has seven guest rooms, all with private baths. This stately house is furnished with period piece antiques and has a large front porch. A complimentary breakfast and afternoon tea are available to the guests. The Admiral Benbow is owned by the Black Dog Tavern Company. Open year-round.

The Admiral Benbow Inn
P.O. Box 24885
20 New York Avenue
Oak Bluffs, MA 02557
☎ *508-693-6825*
$$$

The Four Gables

The Four Gables is situated in a lovely older home and was recently renovated. Much care has been made in restoring the Inn, built in 1896. The Inn's four rooms are nicely decorated with antiques and beds with canopies of netting. Several of the rooms have private balconies. Rocking chairs line the veranda. There's a croquet set, bicycles and board games for your entertainment. A continental breakfast is served daily. Open throughout the year.

Four Gables
41 New York Avenue
P.O. Box 1441
Oak Bluffs, MA 02575
☎ 508-696-8384
$$$

The Dockside Inn

Overlooking the Oak Bluffs Harbor, the Dockside Inn has considerable charm and is wonderfully located. This three-story inn offers its guests all of the amenities of modern living amid turn-of-the-century atmosphere. Cheerful flowered wallpaper and delicate draperies give the rooms a sense of whimsy. Many rooms have a view of the harbor. The inn offers a complimentary breakfast in the private garden or on the front porch. The brochure quotes a couple who wrote about their honeymoon: "Thanks for the spoiling. We are starting our life together here..."

The Dockside Inn
Circuit Avenue Extension
P.O. Box 1206
Oak Bluffs, MA 02557
☎ 508-693-2966 or 800-245-5979
Fax 508-696-7293
http://vineyard.net/inns
$$$

Restaurants

Lola's

One of the nicest restaurants on the Island, Lola's is known for its tasty Cajun seafood specialties. Choose from seafood jambalaya, blackened grilled shrimp and other Southern favorites. Their garlic mashed potatoes are out of this world. The restaurant also offers a bountiful Sunday brunch. For a lighter, less-expensive meal, consider eating at Lola's bar restaurant, which offers nightly music entertainment throughout the summer.

Lola's
Beach Road
Oak Bluffs, MA 02557
☎ *508-693-5007*
$$$

Zapotec

Delight in south-of-the-border specialties at this funky but fun restaurant. Choose from enchilada chicken itza, pollo suiza de los santos and other Mexican food favorites. Located near downtown, one block east of Circuit Avenue.

Zapotec 10
Kennebec Avenue
Oak Bluffs, MA 02557
☎ *508-693-6800*
$$

The Sweet Life Café

A recent addition to Oak Bluffs, the Sweet Life Café offers its guests an intimate dining experience. The patio is very romantic. Enjoy freshwater blue pawns, roasted red pepper cod and other seafood. Or consider the café for a Sunday brunch.

The Sweet Life Café
168 Circuit Avenue
Oak Bluffs, MA 02557
☎ *508-696-0200*
$$$

Jimmy Seas Pan Pasta Restaurant

If the local Islanders were rating restaurants, Jimmy Seas would win first place. The pasta couldn't be fresher. Each dish is pan-cooked to order. Favorites include tagliatelle pomodoro, lobster fra diavolo and other seafood pastas. There's often a long wait for service, but it's well worth it. The restaurant is located near downtown in a small and rather funky old house. It has a down-home atmosphere but is definitely a gastronomical delight.

Jimmy Seas
32 Kennebec Avenue
Oak Bluffs, MA 02557
☎ *508-696-8550*
$$$

The Stand By Café

This small and intimate café looks like the interior of an old railroad car. Recently transformed from a diner to a first-rate dining experience, this family run café has tasty breakfasts, lunches, and dinners. Dinners include such fare as pan-roasted halibut with a carrot ginger sauce, and pan-seared salmon with mashed potatoes, sauteed plum tomatoes and fresh basil in a thyme-infused sauce.

The Standby Café
7 Oak Bluffs Avenue
Oak Bluffs, MA 02557
☎ *508-696-0220*
$$$

Martha's Vineyard

Linda Jean's Restaurant

Definitely an Island institution, this is the quintessential coffee house, with food reminiscent of the 1950s. Open for breakfast, lunch, and dinner, the only problem with the restaurant is its popularity. Be prepared to wait up to an hour for seating.

Linda Jeans
34 Circuit Avenue
Oak Bluffs, MA 02557
☎ *508-693-4093*
$

Brasserie 162

A newcomer to Oak Bluffs, Brasserie 162 is by far one of the most elegant restaurants. Specialties include shrimp martini (spice-rubbed shrimp served atop garlic mashed potatoes), grilled free-range chicken breast marinated in yogurt and Moroccan spices, and other gourmet delights. Reservation srecommended.

Brasserie 162162
Circuit Avenue
Oak Bluffs, MA 02557
☎ *508-696-6336*
$$$$

City Ale and Oyster

Also a new addition to Oak Bluffs, the City Ale and Oyster hosts a restaurant with an extensive seafood and meat menu, plus a small brewery. Complete with its own Brew Master, City Ale and Oyster offers eight Vineyard beers on tap. It's just a block away from downtown Oak Bluffs, on the corner of Kennebec and Healy Avenue.

City Ale and Oyster
Kennebec Avenue
Oak Bluffs, MA 02557
☎ *508-693-2626*
$$$

Other Eateries

Enjoy freshly brewed coffee and an assortment of pastries at a local Island favorite, **Mocha Motts**. *Mocha Motts, Circuit Avenue,* ☎ *508-696-1922.* **The Old Stone Bakery** offers fresh-baked goods, and the best apple fritters on the Island (possibly the world). It also has a small selection of sandwiches available. *The Old Stone Bakery, Park Avenue (next to the Oak Bluffs Post Office),* ☎ *508-693-3668.*

Touring Oak Bluffs

Welcome to Oak Bluffs, the home of the magical Methodist Camp Grounds and more. Begin your tour at the **Camp Grounds**, just a block west of Circuit Avenue. The tiny rainbow-colored cottages are built in a circle facing the Tabernacle. They were built in the mid-19th century. Fueled with something bordering on religious fervor, the owners began to design the cottages, each one more ornate than the previous one. Each cottage is unique with every imaginable whimsy brought to the finished product. Take a moment to look at the intricate jigsaw scroll work on the roof and eaves, the Gothic Revival windows and doors with pointed arches.

Many of the cottages have been owned by the same family since they were built, passed down from generation to generation. You can tour the interior of a Camp Ground cottage at the Cottage Museum, located at 1 Trinity Park. Open throughout the season, the museum houses Camp Grounds memorabilia and antiques. Contact Kathy McKenzie at the Camp Meeting Association for museum hours, ☎ 508-693-0525.

The **Tabernacle** is the central focus of the Camp Grounds. Built in 1879, it is one of the largest wrought iron structures in the United States and is listed on the National Register of Historic Places. The Tabernacle continues to hold religious services and also hosts a number of musical and cultural events.

> *President Clinton and his family often attend
> the Tabernacle's Sunday services during their
> Vineyard vacations.*

Also in the Camp Grounds is the **Trinity Methodist Church**.
Built in 1878, the church features beautiful stained glass windows.

Get in touch with your inner child at the **Flying Horses Carousel**, located at the foot of Circuit Avenue. This famous carousel is one of the oldest in the country, and the wooden horses are more than a century old. If you are lucky enough to capture one of the brass rings, you'll win a free second ride. The carousel belongs to the Martha's Vineyard Preservation Trust and is listed on the National Register of Historical Places. Open 10am-10pm daily, spring through fall.

There's never a dull moment on **Circuit Avenue**, the main street running through Oak Bluffs. There's a full array of shops, from elegant boutiques to the down home curio shops. At the end of the avenue and to your left, you will find the **Union Chapel** (☎ 508-693-5350), built in 1871. Take note of the domed ceiling and triangular windows, which gives the church its uniqueness. Non-denominational services continue to be held here. The church also hosts a variety of concerts and other cultural events throughout the year.

Also take note of the Queen Anne architectural style of the nearby homes. The houses are built in a hodgepodge of styles, many with irregular roof lines, bay windows, dormers and cupolas.

During the later part of the 19th century, Oak Bluffs became a popular summer vacation spot with African-American Bostonians, eventually drawing African-Americans from New York, Philadelphia, and Washington. The area continues to attract African-American tourists and residents.

Ocean Park, just east of downtown, is a wide-open space with many events taking place throughout the summer. The park's gazebo serves as a bandstand every other Sunday afternoon in season. As you stand in the park, imagine Oak Bluffs during its heyday. A gigantic music and dance hall called **The Tivoli** ("I lov it" spelled backwards) stood nearby, a two-story structure with a tower on each end, painted a bright yellow with a red trim. A train called *The Active* ran from Edgartown to Oak Bluffs and the five-story Sea View Hotel overlooked the waterfront. Unfortunately, many of Oak Bluff's original buildings were destroyed in several fires in 1892. Spared from the fire, and an excellent example of the town's former incarnation, is the four-story, gingerbread-trimmed **Wesley Hotel**. Located across from the harbor, the hotel has been a part of Oak Bluffs landscape for over a hundred years.

Be sure to walk along the bustling **Oak Bluffs Harbor**, where you'll find yachts, fishing boats and ferry services. Several pleasant eateries overlook the water.

Spectacular views are around each corner in the **East Chop** area, just a short distance from Oak Bluff's downtown. The **East Chop Lighthouse** offers panoramic views of the Sound and Cape Cod. The lighthouse was built in 1875 and is open to the public on Sunday evenings throughout the summer.

Outdoor Fun

Beaches

Oak Bluffs Beach: Located on either side of the ferry terminal, Oak Bluffs Beach is easily accessible, offering shallow and calm waters. Because of its close access to Oak Bluffs, it can get rather crowded.

Joseph Sylvia State Beach: This two-mile expanse of sand is located between Oak Bluffs and Edgartown, along Beach Road. Parking is available on Beach Road. A bicycle path between Edgartown and Oak Bluffs will take you to the beach.

At the bridge between Oak Bluffs and Vineyard Haven is Eastville Beach, a small beach area, just about a half-mile outside of Oak Bluffs downtown area. It's good for swimming or fishing.

Parks, Preserves and Forests

Lobster Hatchery and Brush Pond can be found just off County Road, on Shirley Avenue. Learn more about the natural habitat and propagation of lobsters. The hatchery is open daily. ☎ 508-696-0552 or 693-0060.

Explore **Crystal Lake**, an 18-acre wildlife and bird refuge owned by the East Chop Association. Just off East Chop Drive, there's something remarkable about seeing this lake on one side of the road, and the Sound on the other.

Vineyard Haven

The commercial center of the Island, Vineyard Haven is the main port of entry for the Steamship Authority and all other commercial boats coming in and out of the area. Vineyard Haven is probably the least distinct of the three down-Island towns, but its charm is in its lack of pomp and circumstance. Main Street is comprised of several nice boutiques, antiques shops, restaurants and jewelry stores.

The residential areas of Vineyard Haven are quite pleasant. You'll enjoy walking through the neighborhood, with tree-lined streets, comfortable houses and carefully tended gardens.

Traveling by foot is still your best option. There is shuttle service to and from the other down-Island towns, and a parking lot is available just outside of downtown (on Highpoint Lane across from Cronigs Market on State Road).

Welcome

Romantic Inns & Hotels

✝ The Thorncroft Inn

The innkeepers here are guaranteed to spoil you. The inn is comprised of two separate homes on 3½ acres of wooded land. There are 14 guest rooms, each with private baths. Four-poster beds, working fireplaces and period antiques give each room a unique charm. There's a private cottage for those romantics seeking absolute privacy. Several rooms have two-person Jacuzzis or a private hot tub. You'll be treated to a full country breakfast and afternoon tea in the lovely dining rooms. Or treat yourselves to a continental breakfast in bed! All rooms are equipped with air-conditioning, phone, color cable television, hairdryer, robes, iron and ironing board. There's evening turn-down service, and morning newspaper delivery. North of downtown, on Main Street. Open all year.

DONNA M. BLACKBURN

The Thorncroft Inn
460 Main Street, P.O. Box 1022
Vineyard Haven, MA 02568
☎ *508-693-3333*
$$$$

Captain Dexter House

If you think it's impossible to travel back in time, you haven't
been to the Captain Dexter House in Vineyard Haven. This elegant restored sea captain's home has all the charm of the past
century, with Edwardian and Victorian furnishings, paintings
and atmosphere. Enjoy freshly squeezed juices, homemade
baked goods and coffee and tea in the stately dining room or
while sitting in the flower garden. The Dexter House has a
great location, just a short walk from downtown Vineyard Haven.

Captain Dexter House
92 Main Street, Box 2457
Vineyard Haven, MA 02568
☎ *508-693-6564*
$$$

Twin Oaks Inn

There is something very cheerful about this Dutch Colonial-style inn. Although located near downtown Vineyard Haven, it has a distinctive country quality. I particularly liked the sitting room patio, filled with country furnishings of pastel pinks, whites, and blues. A lovely private garden area adjoins the building. Continental breakfast is served daily. Open throughout the year.

Twin Oaks Inn
8 Edgartown Road
P.O. Box 1767
Vineyard Haven, MA 02568-1767
☎ 800-696-8633
$$$

✈ Martha's B&B Place

DONNA M. BLACKBURN

Romantic and elegant, this Greek Revival home is picture-perfect. Every effort has been made to give this inn its special historic feel, from the crystal chandeliers to the Persian carpets and antique furnishings. Several suites have working fire-places, harbor views and private Jacuzzis. Enjoy a daily break-fast and an afternoon tea. Martha's also offers nightly turn-down service. Conveniently located near downtown Vine-yard Haven, on Main Street. Open all year.

Martha's B&B Place
114 Main Street
P.O. Box 1182
Vineyard Haven, MA 02568
☎ *508-693-0253*
$$$$

Ocean Side Inn

Just a hop, skip, and a jump from downtown Vineyard Haven, this wonderful location can't be beat. The inn's two acres of wa-terfront property offer panoramic views of the harbor and its own private beach. There are honeymoon and anniversary ac-commodations in its penthouse suite. All rooms are air-conditioned and have private baths. A continental breakfast is served on the deck each morning.

Ocean Side Inn
P.O. Box 2700
105 Main Street
Vineyard Haven MA 02568
☎ *508-693-1296*
$$$

Restaurants

Before reviewing the restaurant section, please note that Vine-yard Haven is a dry town. Alcoholic beverages are not served at any of the restaurants. However, you can bring your own bever-ages.

The Black Dog

By far the most famous of restaurant on the Island, The Black Dog celebrated its 25th birthday in 1996. It has several locations now, but the original Black Dog is located on the beach, off the Five Corners in Vineyard Haven. Choose from an assortment of local seafood and other delights while dining overlooking the harbor. Its rustic, wood interior gives it its New England charm. The Black Dog serves breakfast, lunch, and dinner. There's usually a wait, so come early.

The Black Dog
Beach Street
Vineyard Haven, MA 02568
☎ *508-693-9223*
$$$

Martha's Vineyard

DONNA M. BLACKBURN

Le Grenier

This French delight offers an intimate, romantic dining experience. The second-floor restaurant exhibits simple elegance with its linen tablecloths and candlelight dining. Owner and chef Jean Dupon brings to the restaurant his magic from his native Lyon, France. By far one of the best restaurants in the area, choose from lobster Normande, roast duck, and other French seafood and meat dishes. Reservations are recommended.

Le Grenier
Upper Main Street
Vineyard Haven, MA 02568
☎ 508-693-4906
$$$$

Stripers

This waterfront restaurant is just a short distance from downtown. Choose from roast cod and roast rack of shrimp with asparagus and other seafood, meat and chicken dishes. The restaurant offers nice views of the harbor and has an open feeling to it. Outdoor seating is also available.

Stripers
52 Beach Road
Vineyard Haven, MA 02568
☎ 508-693-8383
$$$

Other Eateries

Located outside of downtown, the **Black Dog Bakery Café** is a pleasant addition to the main restaurant's offerings. It offers breakfast, lunch, and dinners with counter and table service available. Enjoy a breakfast pastry with a hot cup of freshly brewed coffee in the morning; a nice selection of sandwiches and hot dishes for lunch; and a variety of fresh seafood and special pasta dishes at dinner time. Because of the Black Dog's popularity, there's often a wait. *Black Dog Café, 157 State Road, Vineyard Haven, MA 02568,* ☎ *508-696-8190. $*

The original **Black Dog Bakery**, located next to the main restaurant, offers a full range of bakery delights and coffees. Behind the bakery is the **Black Dog General Store**, where you can buy their famous T-shirt and other logo items.

The Vineyard Gourmet has a splendid selection of picnic baskets and boxed lunches, as well as a full summer take-out menu. They also offer full catering service. Choose from gourmet sandwiches, salads, coffees, teas, and cheeses. *Vineyard Gourmet, Main Street, Vineyard Haven, MA 02568,* ☎ *508-693-5181. $*

Touring Vineyard Haven

As with any of the down-Island towns, travel on foot is the best way to see Vineyard Haven. The first white inhabitants of Vineyard Haven settled in 1674. Vineyard Haven has two names: Vineyard Haven and Tisbury. This will confuse any new visitor to the area. The town was initially called Holmes Hole and was a village within the township of Tisbury. In 1871, the town broke away from Tisbury and changed its name to Vineyard Haven. Later, it changed its name to Tisbury. While most people recognize the town as Vineyard Haven, old-timers continue to call the town Tisbury.

Vineyard Haven was a major seaport throughout the 19th century. While the town has maintained much of its earlier flavor, a fire ripped through it in 1883, destroying many of the buildings.

The **Tisbury Town Hall**, ☎ 508-696-4200, located on Spring Street, was built in 1844 and was initially a Congregational Meetinghouse. Its second floor houses the Katherine Cornell Memorial Theater. The theater offers year-round entertainment, including plays, concerts, lectures, and community events. Take note of the theater's murals portraying Island history, painted by local artist Stan Murphy.

By far the most elegant street in Vineyard Haven and a part of the National Historic District is **William Street**, a block east of downtown. Many of the homes are from the Greek Revival era, built during Vineyard Haven's prosperous seaport days.

At the corner of Williams and Church is the **Vineyard Playhouse**, ☎ 508-693-6450; box office, ☎ 508-696-6300. This handsome two-story building was recently renovated and offers good, professional theater, including first run, avant garde, and old standard favorite productions.

At the corner of Main Street and Colonial Lane, you'll find the **Daughters of the American Revolution Building**. Take a moment to read the plaque on the flagpole which commemorates an act of defiance made by three village girls during the Revolutionary War. These brave souls single-handedly blew up a liberty pole using gunpowder to prevent its capture by the enemy British forces.

Just above downtown, on Main Street, is **Owen Park**. The park has pleasant views of the harbor and a small stretch of beach. The bandstand here is used throughout the summer for concerts and other community events. There are plenty of beautiful homes, wonderful views of the Sound and the West Chop Lighthouse, just above Vineyard Haven's downtown area. At the turn of the century an influx of wealthy Bostonians built their summer homes there. Since then, many other people have made West Chop their home, including several celebrities.

The **West Chop Lighthouse** was built in 1817. The original wooden lighthouse was replaced by the present brick structure in 1838. In typical Vineyard fashion, the locals couldn't make up their minds where the lighthouse should be. It was moved twice, once in 1848 and again in 1891. The Coast Guard currently occupies the small caretaker's cottage on the lighthouse premises.

Outdoor Fun

Beaches

Owen Little Way Town Beach (Tisbury Town Beach):
Just moments away from Vineyard Haven, this small stretch of
shorefront is nice for swimming and sunbathing. There's limited parking, but it's right next to town, with access from Main
Street. Located at the end of Owen Lane Way, next to the Vineyard Haven Yacht Club.

Owen Park and Beach: This harbor beach also offers quick
access to Vineyard Haven. Situated at Owen Park on Main
Street.

Lake Tashmoo Town Beach: You won't have to battle the
crowds at this small sandy beach (just 2.5 acres), overlooking
the Vineyard Sound. Take Franklin Street to Daggett Avenue
and turn left. Follow the road to the end of Herring Creek Road.

Forests, Parks & Preserves

There are nine acres of forest preserve near Lagoon Pond in
Brightwood Park. A short trail leads you through the area.
Access through the Martha's Vineyard Land Bank's Ramble
Trail Preserve at the end of Weaver Lane on Hines Point.

The **Shellfish Hatchery** is a marine research and propagation center off Winyah Lane. Stairs lead down to the lagoon and
a dock.

Tisbury Meadow Preserve: Owned by the Land Bank, these 83 acres offer paths for horseback riding and hiking. It's located off State Road, 0.4 miles past the Lake Tashmoo Overlook.

With easy access from Vineyard Haven, the 90-acre **West Chop Woods Preserve** features trails through oak and pine trees. **West Chop Meadow**, located to the northeast, has an expansive view of the outer harbor, East Chop, and beyond. Bring a picnic basket! Follow Franklin Avenue about .4 miles past Daggett Avenue to reach the preserve.

Up-Island

Up-Island is remote, beautiful, and less crowded than the rest of the Island. You'll find forests, ponds, lakes, rolling hills, farm animals, wildlife, and spectacular views of the sea. The towns which comprise Up-Island (West Tisbury, Chilmark, Menemsha, and Gay Head), are small and quaint. They represent a view of New England as it once was. Most people will need a car to get to this part of the Island, but it's also accessible to heartier bicyclists.

West Tisbury

West Tisbury is the first Up-Island town past Vineyard Haven. It was my home for several years. There was nothing more wonderful than waking up to a field of snow in the winter, seeing the first flowers in spring and spending lazy days at the beach in summer. Its rural beauty is quite phenomenal.

Romantic Hotels & Inns

The Bayberry Hotel

Rosalie Powell, the innkeeper here, is a 13th-generation Mayhew who has lived on the Island for a number of years. The house was built in 1969, but was designed to look like a 17th-century farm house.

There are five bedrooms, four with private baths. Each room is cheerfully decorated with floral wallpaper, soft rose and blue bed linens, and antiques. The honeymoon room has a king-size bed, blue and white wallpaper, lovely lace curtains, and a private bath.

You can enjoy homemade food while sitting on the terrace overlooking a carefully tended garden. The breakfast menu changes daily. You'll be able to use a guest pass to the West Tisbury beaches.

The Bayberry
Old Courthouse Road
P.O. Box 654
West Tisbury, MA 02575
☎ 508-693-1984
$$$

⚥ The Lambert's Cove Inn

This beautiful inn offers the best in country living. Far from the madding crowd, this inn's 13 rooms overlook garden and forest. The main building has a wonderful library, a restaurant, and living room. The upstairs guest rooms are cheerfully decorated with antique and wicker furniture.

Several buildings on the property have guests' quarters with private porches. It's the perfect place for a wedding (I know first-hand, my sister was married here!).

DONNA M. BLACKBURN

A full complimentary breakfast is served during the season, the restaurant is open for dinner to the general public through-out the year. The inn provides passes to the West Tisbury beaches for guests.

> *The Lambert's Cove Inn*
> *Lambert's Cove Road*
> *RFD Box 422*
> *Vineyard Haven, MA 02568*
> ☎ *508-693-2298*
> *$$$*

Restaurants

Remember, alcoholic beverages are not served at any of the restaurants. However, you can bring your own beverages.

Lambert Cove Inn Restaurant

The restaurant at the Lambert Cove Inn is excellent. The dining room, in keeping with the tradition of the inn, is cheerful, tastefully decorated and airy. Choose from an assortment of seafood and meat dishes, including pan-seared peppered swordfish or three-cheese spinach ravioli. The restaurant also offers an excellent Sunday brunch. Bring your own alcoholic beverages. Reservations are recommended.

Lambert's Cove Inn Restaurant
Lambert's Cove Road
Vineyard Haven, MA 02568
☎ 508-693-2298
$$$$

The Red Cat

This small café has expanded its menu in the past couple of years. It is open for lunch and dinner. Seating is available in a small dining room or in a screened porch area. There's a down-home atmosphere, and the food is good. The dinner menu offers seafood specialties and other tasty items.

The Red Cat
State Road
West Tisbury, MA 02575
☎ 508-693-9599
$$$

Other Eateries

Located next to the Alley General Store, **Back Alley's Bakery** has a nice selection of sandwiches, pastries, and coffees. A good choice for picking up lunch items for a romantic picnic. *Back Alley's, State Road, West Tisbury, MA 02575,* ☎ *508-693-7366. $*

Next to the West Tisbury Post Office, the **Biga** bakery/café offers a variety of sandwiches and pastas, pastries and breads. There's a pleasant patio outside. *Biga, State Road, West Tisbury, MA 02575,* ☎ *508-693-6924. $*

Martha's Vineyard

Also in the West Tisbury area are several bakeries. Stop in for a pastry and coffee in the morning, or an afternoon dessert for your sweet tooth. One favorite is **The Scottish Bakehouse**, *State Road, West Tisbury, MA 02575,* ☎ *508-693-1873.* Also try **Humphries Bakery**. *Humphries Bakery, State Road, N. Tisbury, MA 02575,* ☎ *508-693-1079.*

Touring West Tisbury

Leading toward the Up-Island area is Lambert's Cove (off State Road on your right). This area has some lovely homes, with open fields and horses. Follow Lambert's Cove Road as it makes a horseshoe back to State Road. The **Nip and Tuck Farm**, on State Road, is a working farm which continues to function as a farm from the last century. Watch the horse-driven plow work the farm's long stretch of pasture. Buy fresh milk and organic produce at the farm's small stand. The Nip and Tuck Farm also offers horse and buggy hay rides.

Past the West Tisbury Post Office is the **Christiantown Memorial to the Praying Indians**. Located on Christiantown Road, the small chapel was the site for services held to convert the Wampanoug Indians to Christianity in the 17th century. An Indian burial ground is just right of the chapel, where the first Indian converts to Christianity are buried.

West Tisbury's small downtown is comprised of a library, an old mill, a police station, a church, a gas station, the old Agricultural Hall, the town hall, and a general store. Surrounding the town are family homes, farms, and plenty of wide open space.

Alley's General Store has been part of the West Tisbury landscape for over a century. It was recently renovated, but has maintained its original flavor. You can buy all sorts of items at the store: from flashlights, camping equipment and gardening tools to food products and Vineyard memorabilia. Take a moment to view the **Congregational Church**, at the Corner of Music Street and State Road. Again, the Vineyarders were confused as to where a building should be placed, and this church was moved from its original location many years ago.

Several captain houses on **Music Street** were built during the whaling era. Music Street was given its name when several of the original owners bought pianos, to show off their money and prestige.

At the intersection of State and the West Tisbury/Edgartown Road, you'll find **The Old Mill**. It was the site of a satinet manufacturing business (an Island wool used to make whalemen's jackets).

The **Old Agricultural Hall** is the home of the **Saturday Market**, where you can buy fresh produce and flowers from nearby farms. The newer Agricultural Hall can be seen from State Road, and is the site of the **Annual Agricultural Fair** and other community events. The construction of the new Agricultural Hall was a community effort, with many Islanders donating time and money. James Taylor and Carly Simon hosted a concert in 1995, with the proceeds going to the building venture.

DONNA M. BLACKBURN

Chilmark & Menemsha

Almost everyone compares this part of the Island to some part of the British Isles. It offers long expanses of open fields with grazing sheep and horses. Old stone walls zig-zag through the landscape. Long driveways lead to beautiful homes and farmhouses, many with sweeping views of the Atlantic Ocean.

Welcome

Romantic Hotels & Inns

Beach Plum Inn

This inn and restaurant has it all, with sweeping views of the ocean at every turn. The carefully tended gardens are among the prettiest on the Island. The inn has its own private beach and tennis courts. Located on eight acres, it has rooms in the main house and several private cottages. The Beach Plum Restaurant has been a long-time favorite with local residents. Open May to October.

The Beach Plum Inn
North Road
Menemsha, MA 02552
☎ *508-645-9454*
$$$$

The Inn at Blueberry Hill

The Inn at Blueberry Hill feels more like a health spa than a hotel. It has a lovely 25-yard lap pool, tennis courts, volleyball, croquet, and horseshoes. The exercise room has cardiovascular and strength training equipment. Personal trainers are available. Relax at the day's end with a massage or facial.

The inn's rooms are airy and tastefully decorated with simple country furnishings. Each room has a private bath, and many come with a deck or balcony. A continental breakfast is included.

Theo's, the inn's outstanding restaurant, offers a variety of seafood and other Island favorites. Open throughout the year.

The Inn at Blueberry Hill
RR1 Box 309
North Road
Chilmark, MA 02535
☎ *508-645-3322 or 800-356-3322*
Fax 508-645-3799
$$$$

❦ The Captain R. Flanders House

The grounds of this bed and breakfast are awesome. A stone wall zig-zags through the farm's 60 acres. Its pond sparkles,

DONNA M. BLACKBURN

and there is a sense of peace as you enter the farmhouse. The house is tastefully decorated with antiques and country furnishings. In addition to the rooms in the farmhouse, there are two private suites. The house offers catering and wedding-planning services. A complimentary breakfast is served daily with fresh homemade breads and muffins, fresh fruits, coffee, tea, and juice. Beach passes are available for guests.

> *The Captain Flanders House*
> *P.O. Box 384, North Road*
> *Chilmark, MA 02535*
> ☎ *508-645-3123*
> *$$$*

Menemsha Inn and Cottages

The Menemsha Inn and Cottages offers an array of accommodations. For the romantic, the six guest suites are wonderfully private. Sit on your own sundeck, dreamily looking out to sea. The light pine furniture is quite attractive. There are also 12 housekeeping cottages and nine rooms in the main building. Complimentary passes to the Lucy Vincent and Squibnocket beaches. Open from June to November.

> *The Menemsha Inn and Cottages*
> *P.O. Box 38B*
> *Menemsha, MA 02552*
> ☎ *508-645-2521*
> *Prices vary*

Restaurants

Theo's

Located at the Inn at Blueberry Hill, this first-rate restaurant offers a "health supportive cuisine." Choose from a variety of Island seafood dishes, served with organic vegetables grown in the Inn's own garden. The four-course dinner menu selections by chef Robin Le-Doux Forte changes daily. Examples of dishes served at the restaurant include black and white sesame seed-crusted native swordfish steak and rosemary and garlic roasted rack of lamb. Reservations are recommended.

Theo's at The Inn at Blueberry Hill
North Road, Chilmark, MA 02535
☎ *508-645-3322*
$$$$

The Home Port

There are two great things about the Home Port: the view and the lobster. It's New England dining at its most traditional. Enjoy a fresh lobster while looking out at the Atlantic Ocean. Or plan your own picnic on the beach by ordering from Home Port's Back Door's take-out menu. Reservations are an absolute must: there's often a two- or three-week advance reservation list during the season.

The Home Port
North Road, Menemsha, MA 02535
☎ *508-645-2679*
$$$$

Other Eateries

At the **Chilmark Store** the counter-service deli offers a variety of sandwiches and Primo's pizzas. There's a great porch outside of the market where you can sit on a rocking chair while munching your goodies. *Chilmark Store, State Road, Chilmark, MA 02535, ☎508-645-3739.* **Larsen's** is just a shack with benches on the side and wooden picnic tables, but it's a great place to cherish the taste of a lobster or plate of clams. The experience will remind you that life is good. Located at Menemsha Harbor. *Larsen's, Menemsha, MA 02535,* ☎ *508-645-2680. $*

Touring
Chilmark & Menemsha

In the early part of this century, Chilmark became a haven for radicals, artists, and writers. Property was inexpensive in Up-Island then, and those who settled there worked on their creative ventures in comparative quiet. The area is now one of the most exclusive parts of the Island, with many celebrity residents. Even the dead are revered here, with many a visitor making the journey to place flowers on John Belushi's grave in the Chilmark Cemetery. Playwright Lillian Hellman is also buried there.

Chilmark's small downtown has a community center, church, schoolhouse, market, and an art gallery. It's open to Chilmark residents only. **Chilmark School** was built in 1860 and continues to teach the Chilmark children from kindergarten until the fifth grade.

The **Methodist Church** is another downtown Chilmark building which has had a location identity problem. Moved from Middle Road to its present location in 1915, this stately white church and steeple continue to hold services and community events.

Follow Menemsha Crossroad to North Road to get to the picturesque **Menemsha Harbor**. This harbor retains much of its original charm and flavor. Watch the fishermen with their expansive nets haul their catch for the day onto the docks. The Coast Guard has a station at the harbor, and there is a public beach nearby.

Gay Head

*T*his 3,400-acre peninsula at the southwestern end of the Island is a very remote but beautiful piece of land, with the Gay Head Cliffs rising majestically.

Welcome

Romantic Inns & Hotels

The Outermost Inn

This establishment has the most amazing views of Gay Head and the Atlantic Ocean beyond. The open feel to the land and the inn itself can take your breath away. Each of the seven rooms has great views, a private bath, full phone service, and television. The wrap-around porch is the perfect place to read a book or just plain relax. A full breakfast is served daily.

> *The Outermost Inn*
> *RR1, P.O. Box 171*
> *Lighthouse Road*
> *Gay Head, MA 02535*
> ☎ *508-645-3511*
> *Fax 508-645-3514*
> *$$$$*

✈ The Up-Island Inn

This is a beautiful Greek Revival-style house in the middle of the country. It is by far one of the most intimate B&Bs on the Island, offering a private and romantic vacation. The three guest rooms are light and airy, with a lovely garden and a beautiful country feel; all have a private bath. You can sense that special care has been taken here. You'll feel totally at home. Open year-round.

The Up-Island Inn
2 Lobsterville Road
Gay Head, MA 02535
☎ *508-645-2720*
$$$

DONNA M. BLACKBURN

Restaurants

The Outermost Inn Restaurant

If you've ever been curious to know the menu choices of the rich
and famous, you should definitely try the Outermost Inn's res-
taurant. The chef, Barbara Fenner, prepares each meal with
care, promising good food made from "the freshest ingredients,
bought, caught and harvested daily and served amid the Out-
ermost Inn's spectacular setting." The seafood platter includes
a whole lobster, stuffed shrimp, steamed littlenecks, scrod,
mussels, broth, and drawn butter.

The Outermost Inn
Lighthouse Road
Gay Head, MA 02535
☎ *508-645-3511*

The Aquinnah

The view can't be beat at the
Aquinnah, located at the Gay
Head Cliffs. Open since 1949,
the Aquinnah restaurant and
gift shop definitely rates as an
Island institution. Serving
breakfast, lunch, and dinner.

The Aquinnah On the Cliffs
Gay Head, MA 02535
☎ *508-645-9654*

Touring Gay Head

The Gay Head Cliffs are a National Landmark. During the sea-
faring days of the 19th century, many references were made to
the cliffs in ships' logs and journals. Above the cliffs is the **Gay
Head Lighthouse**. The first lighthouse was a wooden structure, built in 1844. In 1856, the larger steel lighthouse was
built and fitted with a multi-prismed Fresnel lens, now on display at the Vineyard Museum. The lighthouse's final transformation took place in 1952, when it was automated. Tours are
offered during the summer.

Gay Head is the home of the Wampanoag Indians. The Wampanoags have lived for over 600 years on the Island. In 1987,
the Wampanoag Tribe Council of Gay Head received a determi-
nation from the Bureau of Indian Affairs that recognizned the
Tribe's own government. Although the number of Wampano-

ags living here has diminished (to about 300), the tribe is an important part of the Island culture.

Up-Island Outdoor Fun

Beaches

Several town beaches are located in the Up-Island area, but most of the beaches are open only to town residents. Inquire at your inn whether guest passes are offered. A star (☆) implies that the beach is restricted to residents or passholders (many B&Bs and summer rental houses offer these).

Gay Head Public Beach: A 10-minute walk from the parking lot ($15 per day). This beach extends from Philbin Beach to just before the Gay Head Cliffs. A very appealing stretch of coastline.

☆ **Lobsterville Beach:** This is a beautiful stretch of beach.

Menemsha Beach: Next to the harbor are 16 acres of beach for swimming and fishing. The beach is owned by the town and parking is limited.

☆ **Lucy Vincent Beach**: Located off a dirt road in Chilmark, there are 2,390 feet of prime south shore beach front at Lucy Vincent Beach. Far away from the maddening crowd, this beach is restricted to Chilmark residents.

☆ **Squibnocket Beach**: A lovely stretch of sandy beach, located on the south shore.

> *The late Jacqueline Kennedy Onassis' Vineyard estate is located near Squibnocket Beach.*

☆ **Lambert's Cove Beach, West Tisbury**: Walk about a quarter of a mile through forest before reaching this lovely beach, which features protected sand dunes and the Sound. Restricted to West Tisbury residents only.

Forests, Preserves & Parks

WEST TISBURY: Cedar Tree Neck Nature Preserve is a beautiful stretch of land, with trails leading through forests, ponds and beach. Picnics, swimming and fishing are not permitted, but it's a great place for a hike. (Follow Indian Hill Road, to the end).

Long Point Wildlife Refuge has it all; woods, marsh, pond, and beaches. This 633-acre refuge has a barrier beach at Tisbury Great Pond, and swimming is and swimming is available at the Long cove and South Beach areas. There's seasonal parking and an entry fee for non-members of the Trustees of Reservations.

Manual F. Corellus State Forest stretches from Edgartown to West Tisbury. There is a very nice bike path which is certainly the safest route for bicyclists riding up-island. There are also nature trails and horse paths.

Sepiessa Point Reservation offers 1.4 miles of frontage on the Tisbury Great Pond with horseback trails and walking trails throughout its 164 acres. Entrance is on Tiah's Cove Road. The reservation is owned by the Land Bank.

Also in West Tisbury is **Mill Pond**. This small pond is at the intersection of the West Tisbury/Edgartown Road. Take a moment to watch the swans sail across the pond's surface.

CHILMARK: Fulling Mill Brook includes 46.6 acres of woods, meadows, brooks, and streams, with access from Middle Road and South Road. Also off Middle Road is the **Middle Road Sanctuary**, owned by the Sheriff Meadow's Foundation. The sanctuary has 110 acres of marked trails through the woods. (One of my favorites areas of the Island!)

The **Peaked Hill Reservation** has the highest elevation on the Island (300 feet) and offers panoramic views of the Atlantic Ocean, Squibnocket Pond and Vineyard Sound. The reservation is owned by the Land Bank with access from Tabor House Road. **Waskosim's Rock Reservation**, off North Road, also presents breathtaking views of the Island along with trails through rolling hills, meadows, and wetlands.

Martha's Vineyard

GAY HEAD: Lobsterville Beach and Cranberry Lands is a beautiful but fragile stretch of beach and dunes with a bird nesting area at Cranberry Lands. Parking is not permitted on Lobsterville Road, so access to this area is quite limited.

Annual Events

June

The Annual Harbor Festival: Located at Oak Bluffs Harbor, this June weekend event is a day-long affair with live music, arts and crafts booths, food, and plenty of action. ☎ 508-693-0085.

July

The Portuguese Holy Ghost Feast: This weekend-long event includes a parade, music, dancing, and food. This is a local favorite. Most of the action takes place at the Portuguese American Club, on Vineyard Avenue, just outside Oak Bluffs. ☎ 508-693-1564.

Fourth of July Parade: Enjoy the small-town atmosphere at Edgartown's annual parade. Local merchants and agencies partake in the fun. You'll watch antique cars, fire trucks, bagpipes, and groups of children as they make their way through Edgartown's main streets. This event is colorful and entertaining. End the day with Independence Day fireworks. ☎ 508-693-0085.

The Edgartown Regatta: Held in mid-July, the Edgartown Regatta is one of the largest sailing events in the area, with several class divisions competing. Also, in mid-July the New

York Yacht Club offers a one-day hurrah in Edgartown. ☎ 508-627-4631.

The Tisbury Street Fair: This event offers fun for all, with plenty of activities taking place throughout the day. This event is usually scheduled shortly after the Fourth of July. It's a street fair in the old tradition. Games, food, arts and crafts, street musicians, and more. ☎ 508-696-4200.

August

Illumination Night: This is by far the most spectacular event of the summer. It started as the Camp Ground's final hurrah, signaling the end of summer. A hundred years later, the tradition continues as the crowd eagerly awaits the time when hundreds of Japanese lanterns are lit around the Camp Ground. Illumination Night has become so popular over the years that the town of Oak Bluffs no longer announces the actual date of the event. It will happen on a Wednesday in August, but that's about all the information you'll be able to derive from any native of Oak Bluffs. The beauty of the occasion is somewhat hampered by the crowds. If you are fortunate enough to be there during this event, I recommend that you arrive early with a picnic dinner. Listen to the concert and wait for that wonderful moment of awesome beauty when all the lanterns are lit at once. ☎ 508-693-0085.

Possible Dreams Auction: This is an Island experience which has gained in popularity over the years. With Art Buchwald as the auctioneer, there's never a dull moment. The proceeds of the auction benefit Martha's Vineyard Community Services. You can bid on all sorts of items: Carly Simon will sing at your own private party, Mike Wallace will give you a tour of the 60 Minutes studio, and more.

Admission is $15, but the bids can be for a lot more! ☎ 508-693-7900.

Fireworks At Ocean Park By The Sea: The most incredible fireworks show you'll ever see. As a myriad fireworks explode over the sky, the audience gasps in wonder. You'll laugh, you'll cry, you'll cover your ears and ask for more. Located at Ocean Park, a band concert precedes the display. This event takes place on a weekend night in August. ☎ 508-693-0085.

The Agricultural Fair: Held in mid-August in West Tisbury, this fair is old-fashioned fun at its best and has been an Island event for over a century. It's everything a fair should be, with horse shows and livestock contests, fair rides and games, a ferris wheel, food and more. The new Agricultural Hall is chock full of jams, homemade pies and vegetables. Art and crafts are on display. ☎ 508-693-4343.

Antique Show: Held in Edgartown, and sponsored by the Edgartown Library, the show draws antique dealers from throughout New England. They offer a full array of antiques for sale, including furniture, china, paintings, and quilts. Call ☎ 508-627-4421 for further details.

September

Tivoli Day Festival: This celebration originated during the hey-days of Oak Bluffs. It includes a day-long street fair on Circuit Avenue. The event also hosts several bicycle races, including a round-the-island race, and shorter races at Ocean Park. The bicycling event is part of the United States Cycling Federation National Prestige Classic circuit. ☎ 508-693-0085.

Oak Bluffs House Tour: Offered through the Cottagers, a local women's club in Oak Bluffs, the annual house tour raises funds for several

Vineyard organizations. Visit six houses and have tea at your final destination. ☎ 508-693-0085.

December

Christmas in Edgartown: This annual event is held the second weekend of the month and is celebrated at many Vineyard locations. Experience Christmas from another era with walking tours, horse and buggy rides, and a parade. ☎ 508-693-0085.

First Night: This New Year's Eve party brings plenty of cultural events throughout the Vineyard. A fireworks display at the Vineyard Haven Harbor ends the evening with a bang. ☎ 508-693-0085.

Recreation

Tennis

Edgartown Town Courts are located behind the Edgartown Fire Department on Robinson Road (no phone).

Martha's Vineyard High School: On the Edgartown-Vineyard Haven Road, about four miles from Edgartown (no phone).

Mattakesett Tennis Club: A private club which offers court rentals, in Katama. ☎ 508-627-9506.

Winning Tennis: Tennis Instruction. ☎ 508-627-9200.

Oak Bluffs Town Courts, on Niantic Avenue (no phone).

Island Inn, on Beach Road in Oak Bluffs. ☎ 508-693-6574.

Farm Neck Golf Club, Farm Neck Way (off County Road), in Oak Bluffs. ☎ 508-693-9728.

Vineyard Tennis Court, Inc., 22 Airport Road, West Tisbury (off the Edgartown/West Tisbury Road). ☎ 508-696-8000.

West Tisbury Town Courts, Old County Road at the grammar school. Reservations must be made a day in advance; stop by the school to book a court.

Bicycling

Enjoy the Island by bicycle. It's an excellent alternative to driving, especially during the summer months when there is considerable traffic. You'll find several bike paths that wind their way around the area. The bike path from **Edgartown to Oak Bluffs** parallels Beach Road and is 5.5 miles in length. Inland, you can follow the seven miles of bike path alongside the **Edgartown-Vineyard Haven Road**, and the 8.5 miles of bike paths between **Edgartown and West Tisbury**.

Chappaquiddick is accessible by bicycle and you'll have a shorter wait for passage on the ferry . It's about three miles to **Cape Pogue and the Wasque Wildlife Sanctuary**, with plenty of beautiful terrain along the way. The **East and West Chop** areas are bicycle friendly, with less traffic and plenty of nice places to stop for a picnic.

Up-Island is also less crowded, but you'll be sharing the road with cars (even though there is a designated bike lane on most of the main streets and roads).

Be sure to follow the laws regarding bicycling. They are there to ensure your safety. All of the down-Island towns have bicycle rental shops. I recommend that you rent a helmet as well.

Boating

Enjoy the tranquility and beauty of boating. Let someone else do the work while you take in views of the Island and ocean on a sailing excursion. Or enjoy being the master of your own destiny by renting a boat.

Martha's Vineyard

Sailing Excursions & Harbor Tours

Mad Max Boat Rentals and Sails: On Edgartown Harbor, Edgartown. ☎ 508-627-7500. Offers a romantic evening cruise on a 60-foot luxury catamaran.

Vela Sailing Excursions: At the Memorial Pier next to the Chappaquiddick ferry in Edgartown. ☎ 508-627-1963. Sailing excursions.

Edgartown Harbor Tours, Main Street (near the Yacht Club), Edgartown. ☎ 508-627-4388. Harbor tours.

Harborside Inn Boat Rentals and Instruction, South Water Street, Edgartown. ☎ 508-627-4321. Offers outboard motor boat and sailboat rentals, plus instruction.

Ayuthia Charters, Vineyard Haven. ☎ 508-693-SAIL. Sailboat charters.

Laissez Faire Charters, Vineyard Haven. ☎ 508-693-1646. Sails aboard a 54-foot Alden ketch.

Gosnold Cruises, Vineyard Haven. ☎ 508-693-8900 or 800-693-8001.

Island Classic Charters (a.k.a. Magic Carpet), Up-Island. ☎ 508-645-2889. Sailboat charters.

The ***Shenandoah****,* Vineyard Haven. ☎ 508-693-1699. Square topsail schooner.

Spindrift Charters, Vineyard Haven. ☎ 508-693-4400.

Wind's Up*,* Vineyard Haven. ☎ 508-693-4252.

Boat Ramps/Marinas

Edgartown Memorial Wharf, ☎ 508-627-4746 or 508-627-6185.

Oak Bluffs Marina, ☎ 508-693-4355.

Vineyard Haven, ☎ 508-696-4249.

Menemsha, ☎ 508-645-2846.

Horseback Riding

Martha's Vineyard Horse Council, ☎ 508-645-3723.

Golf

Farm Neck Golf Club: An18-hole golf course off County Road, on Farm Neck Way. Enjoy a tasty meal at the Farm Neck Golf Club Café. ☎ 508-693-3560 (café); 508-693-3057 (club).

Mink Meadows: Nine holes in Vineyard Haven (off Franklin Road). ☎ 508-693-0600.

Entertainment

Movies

A recent addition to Edgartown is the movie complex, **Entertainment Cinemas**, Edgartown 1 & 2. View first run movies in air-conditioned comfort and Dolby sound stereo. Call theater for current movies and show times. Entertainment Cinema, Edgartown 1 & 2, 65 Main Street, Edgartown, MA 02539 ☎ 508-627-8008.

For movie information for any of the theaters below, call ☎ 508-627-MOVY (6689).

Capawock Theater (Vineyard Haven), open year-round.

Strand Theater (Oak Bluffs), late spring to early fall.

Island Theater (Oak Bluffs), late spring to early fall.

Performing Arts

Martha's Vineyard Playhouse, 24 Church Street, Vineyard Haven, ☎ 508-693-6450. Professional theater.

Wintertide Coffeehouse, Five Corners, Vineyard Haven, ☎ 508-693-8830. A community-supported coffeehouse offering music and plays.

The Yard Inc., P.O. Box 405, Chilmark, ☎ 508-645-9662. Dance colony providing performances on the Island.

Martha's Vineyard Chamber Music Society, P.O. Box 4189, Vineyard Haven, MA 02568, ☎ 508-645-9446. Performs throughout the summer at various locations.

The Whaling Church Performing Center, 89 Main Street, Edgartown, MA 02557, ☎ 508-627-4442. Concerts, plays, and lectures.

The Tabernacle, Oak Bluffs, MA 02557, ☎ 508-693-0525. Concerts and lectures throughout the summer.

Music

From classical to rock and roll, a full range of music venues are available at the following locations. Call or consult the local newspapers for further details.

Edgartown

The Seafood Shanty, 31 Dock Street, ☎ 508-627-8622. Jazz, piano or Broadway show music.

David Ryan's Restaurant and Café, 11 N. Main Street, ☎ 508-627-4100. Jazz or Rock 'n Roll.

Hot Tin Roof, at Martha's Vineyard Airport, ☎ 508-693-1137. Rock 'n Roll.

Oak Bluffs

Atlantic Connection, Circuit Avenue, ☎ 508-693-7129. Rock 'n Roll.

The Ritz Café, Circuit Avenue, ☎ 508-693-9851. Rock 'n Roll.

Seasons, Circuit Avenue, ☎ 508-693-7129. Rock 'n Roll.

The Lampost, Circuit Avenue, ☎ 508-693-9352. Rock 'n Roll.

Lolas, Beach Road, ☎ 508-693-5007. Rock 'n Roll, jazz, eclectic.

David's Island House Restaurant and Lounge, Circuit Avenue, ☎ 508-693-4516. Jazz and Broadway show music.

Bus Tours & Charters

Martha's Vineyard Sightseeing, ☎ 508-627-8687.

Gay Head Sightseeing, ☎ 508-693-1555.

Island Transport, ☎ 508-693-0058.

Several other tours are worth mentioning. For a more intimate tour of the Island, consider **Jon's Taxi**, (☎ 508-627-4677). Jon Taxi promises to show you the "hidden beaches on the way to the Menemsha fishing village used in the movie *Jaws*, the Gay Head Cliffs and so much more."

Writer, local celebrity and historian **Holly Nadler** conducts private walking tours through Edgartown, Oak Bluffs, and Vineyard Haven. She's the official "ghost lady" on the Island. (Yes, it's true, the Island is haunted.) Most of the ghosts are friendly. Take a tour of Edgartown with her and she'll share with you the ghosts stories of the Island, from her book, *Haunted Island, True Ghost Stories from Martha's Vineyard*. Other tours include her 'Stories of the Rich and Famous and Dead of Martha's Vineyard' and more. By far the most original storyteller on the Island, she has an insider's point of view. Call Holly at ☎ 508-693-9321.

Transportation

There's no simple way to get to the Vineyard, and during the summer months you can expect traffic to be a problem. It's best to plan your vacation so that you arrive on a weekday, when there is less traffic. No matter what, if you are arriving by car or bus, you should give yourself a little bit of extra time (up to a couple of hours) during the summer.

If you are going to stay in one of the down-island towns (Edgartown, Oak Bluffs, Vineyard Haven), you might want to consider not taking a car. There are several parking lots in New Bedford, Falmouth, and Hyannis. There's shuttle service from Oak Bluffs and Vineyard Haven to Edgartown, so conceivably, you wouldn't need a car. Additionally, it can be difficult to obtain a ferry ticket for your vehicle. By early January of each year, vehicle passes are often sold for the summer. The Steamship Authority has yet to settle on a system that works. At present, there are certain times in which you must have a reservation (primarily the weekends and holidays). Even if you attempt stand-by during the week, you run the risk of very long waits. So plan you trip early, park your car on the mainland or take a plane or bus. There are several car rental agencies on the Island:

AAA Island Auto Rental, Edgartown, ☎ 508-627-6800.

Adventure Rentals, Vineyard Haven, ☎ 508-693-1959.

All-Island Rent A Car, Martha's Vineyard Airport, ☎ 508-693-6868.

Atlantic Rent A Car, Vineyard Haven, ☎ 508-693-0480.

Cineyard Rent A Car, Vineyard Haven, ☎ 508-693-9780.

Bayside Auto Rental, Tisbury, ☎ 508-693-4777.

Budget Rent A Car: Edgartown, ☎ 508-627-4900; Oak Bluffs, ☎ 508-693-1911; Martha's Vineyard Airport, ☎ 508-693-7322.

Classic Car Rentals, Vineyard Haven, ☎ 508-693-1833.

Holmes Hole Car Rentals & Limo Service, Tisbury, ☎ 508-693-8838.

Old Colony Service Corp: Edgartown, ☎ 508-627-4728; Martha's Vineyard Airport, ☎ 508-693-2402.

Hertz, Martha's Vineyard Airport, ☎ 508-693-2402.

Thrifty Car Rental, Vinyard Haven, ☎ 508-693-8143.

Vineyard Classic Car, Oak Bluffs, ☎ 508-693-5551.

Vineyard Enterprises, Oak Bluffs, ☎ 508-692-2232.

Martha's Vineyard

By Car & Limo

From New York: Take Route 95 through Connecticut and Rhode Island. From Providence, take I-195 East. At Bourne, take Route 25 East (I-195 South) over the Bourne Bridge, to Route 28 South and to Woods Hole.

From Boston: Take Route 3 to the Sagamore Bridge. Follow Route 6 West to Route 28 South, to Woods Hole. Or follow I-95 to Route 24 and on to I-495 to Buzzards Bay (Bourne). Cross the Bourne Bridge to Route 28 South, which takes you to Woods Hole.

For a romantic evening on the Island, consider using the services of **Muzik Limousine Service & Silver Cloud Coach,** ☎ 508-693-2212. You'll ride in a carefully restored Rolls Royce or a private limousine, perfect for weddings or private tours. The service also can get you to destinations in and around Boston and from New York to Maine.

DONNA M. BLACKBURN

Ferry Services

Several ferry service is available to the Island. The primary company is the **Steamship Authority**, providing passenger and vehicle service from Woods Hole to Oak Bluffs and Vineyard Haven. The other ferry services (from Hyannis, New Bedford, and Falmouth) provide passenger service only. The Steamship Authority, Advance Reservations ☎ 508-693-9130 or ☎ 508-477-8600. The ferry takes 45 minutes, with ferries running throughout the day and evening.

The *Island Queen*, ☎ 508-548-4800. Runs from Late May until mid-October. Passenger service from Falmouth to Oak Bluffs, throughout the day and evening. Travel time is 35 minutes.

Falmouth to Edgartown Ferry, ☎ 508-548-9400. Runs from May through October. Passenger service from Falmouth to Edgartown. Several trips daily.

Cape Island Express Lines, Inc. (Schamonchi), New Bedford ☎ 508-997-1688; www.mvferry.com. Runs from mid-May to mid-October. Passenger service from New Bedford to Vineyard Haven. Several trips to and from the Island throughout the day and evening.Travel time is 1½ hours.

Hy-Line Cruises, ☎ 508-778-2600. Hyannis to Oak Bluffs. Several trips daily throughout the day and evening during the summer months. One hour 45 minutes travel time.

Hy-Line Cruises, ☎ 508-693-0112. Service from Oak Bluffs to Nantucket. Three trips per day from each location. Travel time is two hours, 15 minutes. Runs from June through September

By Plane

Cape Air offers service from Boston, Hyannis, and Nantucket. ☎ 800-352-0714.

US Air Express services Hyannis, Nantucket, New York, and Washington, D.C. (seasonal). ☎ 800-428-4322.

Continental Express flies from Newark, New Jersey on a seasonal basis. ☎ 800-525-0280.

Charter Services

Air New England, Inc., ☎ 508-693-8899.

Direct Flight, Inc., ☎ 508-693-6688.

Ocean Wings Air Charter, ☎ 508-693-5942 or 800-253-5039.

By Bus

Bonanza Bus, ☎ 800-556-3815. Daily service from Logan Airport and South Station in Boston to Woods Hole, and from New York City and Providence to Woods Hole and Hyannis.

A new service will be available as of July 1st, 1998. A train will run from South Station to Kingston, where passangers will transfer onto a bus heading to Woods Hole. Contact the MBTA for train information (☎ 617-222-3200, 800-392-6100). Bus service is through Plymouth & Brockton Street Railroad Company (☎ 508-746-0378). As of press time, no fare or scheduling information was available.

Shuttle Bus Service

Martha's Vineyard Transportation Services, ☎ 508-693-1589 or 508-693-0058 (town-to-town service). Shuttle service from Edgartown, Vineyard Haven, and Oak Bluffs all day until midnight throughout the summer season. Buses pick up every 15 minutes.

Shuttle bus stops are as follows: Vineyard Haven, across from Steamship Authority Terminal and across from Pier 44 on Beach Road; Oak Bluffs, near the civil war statue in Ocean Park; Edgartown, Church Street across from the Old Whaling Church. Up-island schedule stops at Chilmark, West Tisbury, Gay Head, and the airport. Call ☎ 508-683-1589 for more information.

Martha's Vineyard Transit Authority, ☎ 508-627-7448, allows you to park outside downtown Vineyard Haven and Edgartown and get shuttle service into town. The Edgartown parking lot is at Robinson Road and "The Triangle" on Vineyard Haven Road and at the village center.Vineyard Haven parking lot is off State Road to downtown and Union Street. One-way fare: 50¢.

South Beach Trolley: Continuous daily service every 15 minutes from Edgartown's Church Street Visitor's Center to South Beach. Fare: $1.50/one way.

For More Information

Martha's Vineyard Chamber of Commerce, ☎ 508-693-0085.

✺

DONNA M. BLACKBURN

The Upper Cape

It's all there, the beautiful beaches, the historical houses, the charming inns and forest. Easily accessible from Boston and New York, the Upper Cape has something for everyone. It is a perfect place to spend a romantic holiday. A general rule of thumb regarding a tour of the Upper Cape is to stay away from the main highways. This may mean slightly longer trips to and from each town, but it's well worth it. Unfortunately, throughout the Cape, the main highways have given rise to urban sprawl. (Several locals asked me not to write this, as they want the back roads to stay less traveled.) For a less hassled trip, stay away from the main routes. Check your map and I'll also supply you with some suggestions.

The back route to Falmouth and Woods Hole area is Route 28A. After crossing the Bourne Bridge, Route 28A can be reached from the Bourne rotary. This will take you through Pocasset and West Falmouth, past scenic ocean views of Buzzards Bay.

Falmouth is the second largest town on the Cape, and although it has grown over the years, it still retains much of its original charm. The Village Green, in the heart of the town, was placed on the National Register of Historical Places in 1996. You will find several lovely bed and breakfasts and inns on the Village Green. Downtown Falmouth has many nice shops and restaurants, and there's a very active harbor and several attractive beaches. Within a short distance from Falmouth you'll find remote areas perfect for a romantic sojourn. Woods Hole, just four miles away, is a world unto itself. To me, Woods Hole is a marine biology think-tank. For over a hundred years, it has been the home of several world-renowned scientific marine laboratories. Woods Hole feels very remote, but therein lies its beauty. I catch my breath every time as I round the last stretch of highway that leads into Woods Hole harbor and ferry terminal.

Mashpee, just north of Falmouth, is governed by the Wampanoag Indians. Over 600 members of the tribe still live in the area. Mashpee also has several new resort communities, including New Seabury and Popponesset.

Sandwich is just across the Sagamore Bridge and is the oldest town on the Cape. The first settlers arrived there in 1627, and while the town now has a population of around 10,000 year-round residents, it has retained much of the charm of an old Colonial village. It's one of my favorites places to visit on the Cape.

DONNA M. BLACKBURN

Woods Hole

Woods Hole is a small harbor town full of old-time charm. At its center is the ferry terminal, with sea vessels traveling to

Martha's Vineyard. You'll find restaurants and shops on Water Street.

During the summer, scientists from around the world come here to research marine life.

Welcome

Romantic Hotels & Inns

The Marlborough Bed & Breakfast

This B&B occupies a charming reproduction of a Cape Cod home. The two-story white house, complete with picket fence, flower gardens, and expansive front and back lawns, offers a peaceful respite from our frantic world. The five guest rooms are tastefully decorated with country favorites. A private cottage in the back yard is perfect for honeymooners who want only each other's company. The back lawn is splendid. A kidney-shaped pool and an English paddle tennis court are available to guests. Enjoy a full breakfast on the back terrace.

The innkeepers are very friendly here, and they'll take the extra time to make sure your stay is exactly what you want it to be. Open year-round.

The Marlborough
320 Woods Hole Road
Woods Hole, MA 02543
☎ 508-548-6218
Fax 508-457-7519
Reservations, ☎ 800-320-2322
$$$

Woods Hole Passage

In the day time, the Woods Hole Passage is a lovely, two-story shingled carriage house and barn with all the charm of a country home. At night, the outside twinkling lights beckon callers to come in and stay for awhile. The living room offers a mix of old and new, with several modern paintings and sculptures capturing the eye. The guest rooms are spacious. There's a tennis court and a lovely back lawn and garden area. A full breakfast is included in the room price. Woods Hole Passage also offers to-go lunches and candlelight dinners for two for an additional charge.

Woods Hole Passage
186 Woods Hole Road
Falmouth, MA 02540
☎ *508-548-9575*
$$$

Restaurants

Landfall

You can't beat the location, next to the Woods Hole Steamship Authority. It's a great place to chow down on New England seafood (lobster, swordfish, and scallops) while watching the ferries come in and out of port. Reservations are accepted.

Landfall
Woods Hole
☎ *508-548-1758*
$$$

Captain Kidd

Also serving New England specialties, this restaurant/bar is a local favorite with plenty of atmosphere.

Captain Kidd
77 Water Street
Woods Hole
☎ *548-8563*
$$$

Dome Restaurant

This restaurant is housed in a Buckminster Fuller geodesic dome. The food is quite good and features seafood and meat specialties. The restaurant overlooks Woods Hole Harbor and Vineyard Sound. Reservations are needed.

Dome Restaurant
539 Woods Hole Road
☎ *508-548-0800*
$$$

Other Eateries

The small **Pie in the Sky Café and Bakery** offers a nice selection of sandwiches and pastries and is a perfect place to pick up a quick lunch or breakfast while waiting for the ferry to Martha's Vineyard. *Pie in the Sky Café and Bakery, 10 Water Street,* ☎ *508-540-5475. $*

Touring Woods Hole

While Woods Hole is known primarily as a community of scientists, it's also a lovely small town with plenty of New England charm. The nearby beaches and forests are basically unspoiled with wonderful views of Vineyard Sound and Martha's Vineyard Island.

Woods Hole's first scientific venture began in 1871 when the National Marine Fisheries Service started to conduct research in fish management and conservation. In 1888, the Marine Biological Laboratory began to provide research and education in marine biology. In 1930, the Woods Hole Oceanographic Institution opened there and in the 1960s the United States Geological Survey's Branch of Geology initiated research in the area. While most of the laboratories are closed to the public, several of the institutions do offer some public access.

The **Woods Hole Oceanographic Institute** (WHOI), is the world's largest oceanographic laboratory and currently offers undergraduate, graduate, and post-graduate studies in conjunction with MIT. Several of WHOI's buildings are located in downtown Woods Hole; the 200-acre campus is nearby. WHOI took part in the successful 1985 U.S./French search for the *Titanic*. Located at 15 School Street, WHOI has a small exhibit center open to the public during the summer season. Call ☎ 508-289-2663 for more information.

The **Marine Biological Laboratory** has one of the finest science libraries in the world. The library has an extensive collection of biological, ecological, and oceanographic literature. The library is not open to the public, but throughout the summer you can go on a guided tour with a retired scientist as your guide. Call ☎ 508-289-7623 for tour information.

The **National Marine Fisheries Service Aquarium** offers 16 separate tanks of regional fish and shellfish. Nicely displayed, with magnifying glasses and dissecting scopes for closer examination, this hands-on aquarium is a nice way for science buffs and curious romantics to spend the day. Located at the corner of Albatross and Water Way. Call ☎ 508-548-7648 for more information.

History buffs should be sure to visit the **Bradley House Museum**, across from the Woods Hole ferry terminal. The mu-

DONNA M. BLACKBURN

seum has more than 200 tapes of oral histories provided by the old-timers in the area, plus diaries, maps, old ships logs, and more. Located at 573 Woods Hole Road, the museum is open throughout the summer. ☎ 508-548-7270.

My very favorite road in the Woods Hole/Falmouth area is Church Street (later becoming Nobska Road). Just past downtown Woods Hole on the right, this road will take you past the **Nobska Lighthouse**. Built in 1876, this impressive 42-foot cast iron tower is situated on a hill overlooking Vineyard Sound. Currently a Coast Guard station, the lighthouse is open to the public only for special tours.

Continue to meander down **Nobska Road** through forest until you reach the Surf Drive and Surf Side Beach. You'll find a row of houses built on stilts (an attempt by house owners to outsmart the sea). The road will eventually take you through one of Falmouth's historical residential areas. It's a great way to avoid downtown Falmouth traffic.

DONNA M. BLACKBURN

The Upper Cape

Falmouth

The Falmouth Bell
Never was there a lovelier town
Than our Falmouth by the sea
Tender curves of sky look down
on her grace of knoll and lea
~ Katherine Lee Bates

Falmouth is a pleasant mid-sized town which has, thankfully, maintained much of its original lure. And it has something for everyone. For the history buff, there are plenty of old houses and churches. Outdoor opportunities abound, whether you choose to go to the beach, take a bicycling trip, or hike through the forests. Falmouth has several attractive nice restaurants and enough shops to fill anyone's shopping fantasies.

Romantic Hotels & Inns

The Village Green, in the heart of downtown Falmouth and registered on the National Historic Register, has some of the most inviting bed and breakfasts and inns in the area. If you've always wanted to stay in a grand old home with all the elegance of the 19th century, then you have arrived at your destination.

✈ Mostly Hall

It's the grandest inn on the Village Green, with rolling lawns front and back. Built in 1849 by Captain Albert Nye, the house was a wedding present for his Southern bride. Captain Nye wanted her to feel as though she were back home, and so the house has many qualities of a Southern plantation. Six guest rooms are furnished with period antiques, oriental accent

DONNA M. BLACKBURN

rugs, four-poster queen-size beds and more. The wonderfully spacious living room is the perfect place for visiting, as is the back wrap-around porch overlooking the gazebo. A full breakfast and an afternoon are served daily. Mostly Hall is perfect for a romantic holiday. Open from March to December.

Mostly Hall
27 Main Street
Falmouth, MA 02540
☎ *508-458-3786 or 800-682-0565*
$$$

✈ The Palmer House Inn

From the very moment you arrive at the Palmer House Inn, you know you've found a New England treasure. This Queen Anne turn-of-the-century home has all of the charm of a by-gone era. The guest rooms are tastefully decorated with Victorian antiques, lacy curtains and quilts, and flowered wallpaper. Romantic moments can be shared in one of the guesthouse rooms, several of which have whirlpool tubs. The inn offers a

DONNA M. BLACKBURN

full breakfast in the formal dining room, complete with lace tablecloths, fresh flowers, fine china, and classical music. Afternoon tea and cookies are also served. Open all year.

The Palmer House
81 Palmer Avenue
Falmouth, MA 02540
☎ *508-548-1230*
Reservations, ☎ *800-472-2632*
Fax 508-540-1878
$$$

The Inn On the Sound

The views from the front guest rooms are panoramic. Departing from the traditional, this romantic escape is tastefully decorated with chic California-style furnishings. Innkeeper Renee Ross owns the inn with her brother. She is an interior decorator, and has obviously cast a wonderful spell over the decor.

The Fiddler's Cove is a wonderful room, painted taupe with white and black accents. The sleeping alcove is cozy. Sit and gaze out at the wide expanse of Nantucket Sound from the room's formal sitting area. Another room with a view, the Oyster Room, also sports black and white accents, with a large mission oak bed. The three-tier front garden overlooks the Sound. A full gourmet breakfast is served daily, offering three baked goods each morning, fresh seasonal fruit, coffees, teas and more.

The Inn On the Sound
313 Grand Avenue
Falmouth, MA 02540
☎ 508-457-9666 or 800-564-9668
www.falmouth-capecod.com / fww / inn.on.the.sound
$$$

Hewins House

Also on the Village Green, the Hewins House is a small, quiet inn that was recently renovated, with careful attention paid to capturing its original Victorian charm. There are plenty of antiques, lace, and period furnishings. Three guest rooms and a pleasant upstairs sitting area are available. Innkeeper Virginia Price is friendly and will make sure that your vacation is exactly as you would like it to be. A full breakfast is served in the Federal-style dining room. Open throughout the year.

The Hewins House
20 Hewins Street
Falmouth, MA 02540
☎ 508-457-4363 or 800-555-4366
$$$

The Village Green Inn

Picture perfect, this elegant Victorian home has great charm. Its picket fence, potted geraniums, and white wicker porch furniture create the sense of a slower, more peaceful era. The guest rooms are tastefully decorated, and all have private baths. Several of the rooms have working fireplaces. A full breakfast is served, with lots of menu choices. Open April to December.

Village Green Inn
40 Main Street
Falmouth, MA 02540
☎ 508-548-5621 or 800-237-1119
Fax 508-457-5051
E-mail vgi40@aol.com
$$$

The Inn at One Main Street

The Inn at One Main Street has a cheerful exterior, with its wide porch, two-story turrets, and lace curtains. It beckons travelers to come and stay in its Victorian elegance. The turret rooms have a particularly romantic feel to them. The Inn offers a full breakfast. Open year-round.

The Inn at One Main Street
One Main Street
Falmouth, MA 02540
☎ 508-540-7469 or 888-AT-1-MAIN
$$

The Shore Way Acres Inn

Experience the benefits of a resort-style vacation at The Shore Way Acres Inn. This hotel offers a spacious front lawn, with inviting outdoor and indoor pools. Choose from a modern conventional hotel room or a carefully restored country sea captain's room. Play a game of croquet, badminton, or volleyball on the hotel's grounds. The inn offers several vacation packages, including a full meal package featuring full candlelight dinners, a Sunday brunch and more.

The Shore Way Acres Inn
Historic Shore Street
Box G
Falmouth Center, MA 02541
☎ 800-352-7100 or 508-540-3000
$$$

Coonamessett Inn

The Coonamessett Inn has been a popular resort in Falmouth since 1953. Its rustic buildings set amid gardens and facing Jones Pond offer a perfect getaway just moments away from Falmouth's downtown. Several of the tastefully decorated suites have views of the pond. The stately lobby and dining room have old-world charm, with potted plants, fresh-cut flowers, and Cape Cod landscape paintings.

> *Coonamessett Inn*
> *311 Gifford Street*
> *Falmouth, MA 02540*
> ☎ *508-548-2300*
> *E-mail cmi.cathi@aol.com*
> *www.capecod.com / coonamessett*
> *$$$*

The Elms

The Victorian Elms has beautiful, award-winning gardens and close proximity to Buzzard's Bay. The nine guest rooms are furnished with country antiques. Romantics will enjoy a stroll through the gardens and its gazebo, the perfect place for a lovers' rendezvous. A continental breakfast is served daily in the breakfast room overlooking the deck and grounds. Open year-round.

> *The Elms*
> *P.O. Box 895*
> *Route 28A*
> *West Falmouth, MA 02574*
> ☎ *508-540-7232*
> *$$*

The Upper Cape

Restaurants

Coonamessett Inn

The main dining room, with hunter green walls and white linen tablecloths, is quite elegant. The small dining room, overlooking a pond and garden, is equally enchanting. The food is excellent, featuring traditional American favorites. Smart-casual dress is expected. Reservations needed.

Coonamessett Inn
311 Gifford
Falmouth, MA 02540
☎ 508-548-2300
$$$

Flying Bridge Inn

This elegant restaurant offers a great view of the harbor. It serves lunch and dinner and features New England seafood and some meat specialties. Music entertainment is offered in the lounge on the weekends. Casual/smart dress. Reservations are not accepted.

Flying Bridge Inn
220 Scranton Avenue
☎ 508-548-2700
$$

Regatta of Falmouth by the Sea

Enjoy beautiful ocean views and a lovely modern dining room tastefully decorated in soft colors. Choose from American and French cuisine while dining by soft lamplight. A perfect choice for romantics. Reservations are necessary.

Regatta of Falmouth by the Sea
217 Clinton Avenue
☎ *508-548-5400*
$$$

The Nimrod

This cozy, romatic restaurant is housed in an 18th-century building. It features several small dining rooms, each with a fireplace. Choose from such entrées as shrimp and scallops lemon alfredo or pan-seared potato-encrusted tuna. The menu fetaures seafood and continental cuisine. The bar offers jazz six nights a week. Reservations are needed.

The Nimrod
100 Dillingham Avenue
☎ *508-540-4132*
$$$

Dom Bistro

This newer restaurant is getting a lot of attention. Pale yellow walls are complemented by tables set with silver. Freshly cut flowers adorn the dining room. Or eat at the marble-topped tables in the lounge. Offerings include French and Northern Italian cuisine. The menu has a variety of pastas and an assortment of fish, fowl and beef dishes.

DONNA M. BLACKBURN

Dom Bistro
327 Gifford Street
☎ *508-548-9861*
$$$

The Upper Cape

Other Eateries

Enjoy gourmet breakfast and lunch items at the downtown **Food for Thought Restaurant and Catering**. *Food for Thought Restaurant and Catering, 37 N. Main,* ☎ *508-548-4498. $*

Laureens bakery/café has a varied menu with outdoor and indoor seating. Located in downtown, it offers a nice respite for travelers. You can opt to order take-out food for a picnic at the beach. *Laureens, 170 Main Street,* ☎ *508-540-9104.*

Touring Falmouth

The Wampanoag Indians were the first settlers in the area now called Falmouth. They named the area Suckanesset, after the plentiful black wampum, beads that are made from quahog shells.

Bartholomew Gosnold, during his travels through the Cape, renamed the area Falmouth after his home port in England. In the 1660s a group of Quakers who were experiencing religious discrimination in other parts of Massachusetts settled in Falmouth; they incorporated the town in 1686.

Like the rest of the Cape, Falmouth took an active part in the whaling enterprises of the 19th century. Many of the historic homes were built by sea captains who made their money in pursuit of the whale.

The **Congregational Church** at the Village Green was built in 1856. Take note of the bell, designed by Paul Revere. The **1790 Julia Wood House** is the home of the **Falmouth Historical Society**. A museum and colonial gardens are located on the grounds. Many historical items are on view, including antique household items, children's clothing, toys and dolls. See the display of antique medical equipment, a well-restored Colonial kitchen, and more.

In back of the museum the **Hallett Barn Museum** houses antique farm items and a 19th-century horse-drawn sleigh. Also on the premises is the **Conant House**, which houses a collection of antique military and nautical wares and a genealogical and historical library. The Historical Society offers guided and self-guided tours of the area. The museums are located at Palmer Avenue and the Village Green. They are open throughout the summer months. Call ☎ 508-548-4857 for more information.

Katherine Lee Bates, made famous by her song *America The Beautiful,* is a Falmouth heroine. Born at 16 Main Street, the Historical Society now owns her home. It's not open to the public, but you can view a plaque commemorating her birth in 1859.

Take a stroll and browse through the many shops on Falmouth's **Main Street**. The downtown area has maintained much of its original charm.

The **Falmouth Harbor** is a bustling port. Watch boats of all different shapes and sizes as they come in and out of the harbor. Hop the *Island Queen* for a day on Martha's Vineyard Island. There are plenty of seafood restaurants around the harbor, offering the perfect excuse to eat some of New England's famous seafood while watching the boats go out to sea.

Across the harbor is **Falmouth Heights**. This is a pleasant area, with several bed and breakfasts offering views of the sea.

In **East Falmouth** you'll find a lovely stretch of historical sea captain's country homes on Davisville Road. This area once was the strawberry-growing capital of the world. Now you can pick your own at several local farms. Farther east is the small village of **Waquoit** and the relatively remote but lovely Waquoit Bay and Washburn Island. Explore the winding roads of North and West Falmouth. Along the shoreline of **Buzzards Bay** are several lovely sandy beaches with warm water. On Route 28A is the historic **Bourne Farm**, a restored 18th-century homestead.

DONNA M. BLACKBURN

Mashpee

A couple miles north, Mashpee is an odd combination of old and new. Mashpee has been the home of the Wampanoag Tribe for thousands of years, but lately the area has seen the construction of a number of condominium resorts. Mashpee is one of the fastest-growing towns on the Cape.

Welcome
Romantic Inns & Hotels

The New Seabury Resort

A community unto itself, New Seabury Resort is the perfect vacation spot for romantics who enjoy a sporty lifestyle. There are 13 separate villages, each with a different theme. You can stay at a traditional New England-style home, or one with a contemporary California feel. It has two 18-hole golf courses. The Blue Championship course is one of the best in the country. In addition to tennis courts (16 in all) there are bicycle and jogging paths and an oceanfront pool. New Seabury has several beaches for its guests.

After spending the day outside, you can dine at the nearby Popponesset Inn. Several nice shops are located in New Seabury. This resort is perfect for those who like stay at just one place and have everything close by.

The New Seabury Resort
Box 549
New Seabury, MA 02649
☎ 508-477-9111 or 800-999-9033
Fax 508-477-9790
$$$$

Restaurants

Popponesset Inn

This waterfront restaurant, located in New Seabury, is one on the area's most popular, with several indoor and outdoor dining rooms. You can't beat the view and the food is good, focusing on New England seafood. There's live music on the weekends. Reservations are not accepted.

Popponesset Inn
Shore Drive West
New Seabury
☎ *508-477-1100*
$$$

The Flume

This popular restaurant is owned by a Wampanoag chief and is decorated with Indian artifacts. It serves lunch and dinner. The menu consists of New England seafood and a variety of meat dishes. Try the Flume's famous Indian pudding for dessert. Reservations are not accepted, so come early.

The Flume
Route 130, Lake Avenue
☎ *508-477-1456*
$$

The Upper Cape

Touring Mashpee

The Wampanoag Indians laid claim to Mashpee centuries before the arrival of white settlers in the late 1600s. It is one of the two Native American townships in the area (the other is Gay Head), with over 600 Wampanoags still living there. The Mashpee Wampanoag Tribal Council has been operating since 1974. The **Wampanoag Indian Museum**, located on Route 130, has a variety of Indian artifacts, including clothing, hunting and fishing wares, baskets, weapons and more. Call ☎ 508-477-1536 for further information.

The **Old Indian Meeting House** continues to be used as a place for worship and is the oldest church on the Cape. It's on Route 28. Call ☎ 508-477-1546, for more information.

DONNA M. BLACKBURN

Sandwich

𝒯his cozy little town is just a stone's throw from the Sagamore Bridge and can be easily accessed from Boston in about 90 minutes. There's plenty of history in Sandwich, the oldest town on the Cape. The downtown is particularly quaint with the Shawme Duck Pond and Grist Mill as its central feature. There are several whimsical places to visit, such as the Thornton Burgess Museum (he was the author of Peter Rabbit stories) and the Sandwich Doll Museum. Nearby is Cape Cod Bay, with wide expanses of beach and sea.

Welcome Romantic Hotels & Inns

✈ The Dan'l Webster Inn

Guaranteed to spoil you, this first-class inn and restaurant offers all of the amenities of modern living while replicating turn-of-the-century charm and style. The suites are particularly romantic. Consider the Dan'l Webster Suite, with a king-size bed, marble bath with skylight, and a two-person step-in Jacuzzi. Or the Robert Tobey Suite, complete with a working fireplace and baby grand piano. Every room here is furnished with an elegant touch, and the gathering rooms near the lobby are warm and cheerful. The outdoor gardens are carefully maintained, and the swimming pool offers the best in summer relaxation. The inn offers a complimentary guest pass to a nearby health club. Open throughout the year.

The Dan'l Webster Inn
149 Main Street
Sandwich Village, MA 02563
☎ 508-888-3622
$$$

The Upper Cape

DONNA M. BLACKBURN

The Belfry Inne and Bistro

The ornate charm of the Belfry Inne and Bistro can't be beat. The three-story Victorian – complete with tower – is whimsical. The eight guest rooms are tastefully decorated, each with private bath. Romantics should take note of the William A. Drew Room, with its hand-painted furniture and French doors leading out to a private balcony. I liked the Martha Southworth Room, which features a hand-turned walnut spool bed and Wedgewood accents. There's a lovely wall mural in the tower bringing back childhood bedtime stories. The inn offers a buffet-style full breakfast daily for guests. Don't miss the romantic restaurant for dinner.

The Belfry Inne and Bistro
8 Jarves Road, P.O. Box 2211
Sandwich, MA 02563
☎ 508-888-8550; Fax 508-888-3922
$$$$

The Inn at Sandwich Center

This elegant establishment is perfectly located in the center of town, just a stone's throw from the historical Town Hall Square and Shawme Duck Pond. It is listed on the National Register of Historical Places and has many of its original features, such as the Keeping Room's beehive oven and circa 1750 fireplace. The five guest rooms are handsomely decorated with period piece antiques and four-poster beds. Several rooms have fireplaces; all have private baths. A continental homemade breakfast is served daily. Open all year.

The Inn at Sandwich Center
118 Tupper Road
Sandwich, MA 02563
☎ 508-888-6958
E-mail innsan@aol.com
www.bfbooks.com / innsan.html
$$$

The Village Inn

This is a particularly nice bed and breakfast, tastefully decorated with plenty of charm and grace. The inn sponsors art workshops throughout the year, and the entire building reflects innkeeper Susan Fehlinger's artistic background. The five guest rooms are large and airy, and the feather comforters couldn't be more inviting. On cool evenings, snuggle up in front of the room's fireplaces with your love. On warm afternoons, there's nothing better than reading a book or visiting with friends on the wrap-around porch overlooking the garden. A full breakfast is served daily in a very handsome dining room. Open throughout the year.

The Village Inn
4 Jarves Street
Sandwich, MA 02563
☎ 508-833-0363 or 800-922-9989
Fax 508-833-2063
E-mail CAPECODINN@aol.com
$$$

The Upper Cape

Dunbar Tea Inn

This bed and breakfast is adjacent to its Tea Shop and offers a pleasant stay in an English country-style inn. The three guest rooms are tastefully decorated with lace, antique furnishings, and quilted bed covers. The inn overlooks the Shawme Pond – a picture-perfect setting. Enjoy a complimentary full breakfast in the morning and then stroll over to the tea room for an afternoon pot of Earl Grey. Open year-round.

The Dunbar Tea Inn
1 Water Street
Sandwich, MA 02563
☎ 508-833-2485
$$

Restaurants

Dan'l Webster Inn Restaurant

A long-time favorite among locals and visitors, the Dan'l Webster Inn Restaurant has a comprehensive New England seafood and meat menu. Several dining rooms comprise the restaurant, including the Conservatory Room, with its plants, twinkling lights and romantic atmosphere. The Music Room is more old-fashioned, with pine paneling, a fireplace, and a grand piano. The Heritage Room is often used for private parties and weddings. For casual dining, consider The Tavern, also panelled, with an original English Colonial flare. Reservations are recommended.

The Dan'l Webster Inn
149 Main Street
☎ 508-888-3622
$$$$

The Belfry Inne and Bistro

The restaurant at the Belfry Inne is wonderfully romantic, with plenty of Victorian charm. The menu features nouvelle cuisine. Choose from entrées like moist and juicy large sea scallops sautéed golden brown and served with roasted cashew and scallion basmati rice, or oven-roasted New England lamb sautéed sage polenta, baby carrots, asparagus and an herbed red wine sauce.

The Belfry Inne and Restaurant
8 Jarves Road
P.O. Box 2211
☎ 508-888-8550
$$$

The Dunbar Tea Shop

Enjoy an English cream tea, a smoked fish platter, and other English delights at this wonderfully quaint and very authentic English tea shop.

The Dunbar Tea Shop
1 Water Street
☎ 508-833-2485
$$

Touring Sandwich

Sandwich is a dream of a town. Nestled below the Sagamore Bridge, it's a great introduction to the Cape. The downtown's picturesque **Shawme Duck Pond** is perfect for a peaceful respite. Here you will find the waterwheel-powered Dexter Grist Mill, built in 1654 and open to the public throughout the summer. Also on the pond is the **Thornton W. Burgess Museum**. Childhood memories will be recalled as you step into the museum's small house. Thorton Burgess wrote more than 170 books, mainly for children. His characters include Peter Rabbit, Reddy Fox and many other famous Old Briar Patch characters. Located at 4 Water Street; ☎ 508-888-4668 for more information.

Across the street is the stately **Church of Christ**, built in 1848. It's a perfect example of a 19th-century church, complete with white exterior and tall spire.

The **Hoxsie House** is also on the pond. It's considered to be the oldest house on the Cape. An old saltbox, it has not been modernized since 1675. Furnished with Colonial pieces on loan from the Museum of Fine Arts in Boston, it's open to the public throughout the summer. Of particular note are the collection of spinning wheels and a 17th-century harness loom. Call ☎ 508-888-1173 for opening times.

In the 19th century, Sandwich was known for its production of glass. Aptly called Sandwich Glass, the intricate beauty of the glass can not be overlooked. Now considered quite valuable by collectors, the **Sandwich Glass Museum** has a beautiful collection of vases, jewelry, dinnerware and more. The displays are instructive, showing the art of glass-making. Don't miss

this museum. Located at 129 Main Street; call ☎ 508-888-0251 for more information.

Get in touch with your inner child at the **Yesteryears Doll Museum**, with its wonderful collection of antique French, German and Chinese dolls. A miniature millinery shop, a Victorian dollhouse and a Henry VIII doll collection (complete with all of his wives) are just some of the delights. Located in the 1833 First Parish Meetinghouse at 143 Main Street. Call ☎ 508-888-1711 for further information.

The Heritage Plantation is considered to be Sandwich's jewel in the crown. Commissioned by the family of Josiah K. Lilly III, (the man who amassed a fortune in the pharmaceutical business), the museum is known for its Americana collection. There's an awesome automobile display which includes President William Howard Taft's White Steamer, Gary Cooper's green-and-yellow Duesenberg and 35 other antique and classic cars. The Art Museum has an impressive collection of Currier and Ives pieces, as well as many antique toys. Take a ride on the carefully restored 1912 Carousel.

A Military Museum is also housed here, complete with a 2,000 piece hand-painted soldier set. The museum's grounds are quite beautiful, offering an abundance of rhododendron and day lily beds, for which it is known. Evening concerts are held in the garden throughout the summer. Located at Grove and Pine Street, the museum is a short walk from downtown. Call ☎ 508-888-3300 for museum and concert information.

The **Sandwich Boardwalk** will take you to Town Neck Beach and is a testament to the town's community spirit. In 1991, Hurricane Bob destroyed the previous boardwalk. The town's people gathered together and donated new planks, each with personal messages. You'll be so absorbed reading the inscriptions that you might forget to take in the panoramic view of Massachusetts Bay. About a mile's walk from downtown (follow Jarvis Street to its end to the boardwalk parking lot).

Another way to see the Cape is by train. Enjoy the **Cape Cod Scenic Railroad**, a two-hour rail excursion past Cape Cod Bay, the Cape Cod Canal, through cranberry bogs and salt marshes. The train travels from Sandwich to Hyannis several times a day, with narrated commentary on the Cape's history and folklore. Also consider the **Cape Cod Dinner Train**, a

gourmet feast billed as a three-hour culinary journey. Call
☎ 508-771-3788.

The Cape Cod Canal Region

Known as the gateway to the Cape, the towns of Sagamore
and Bourne are situated adjacent to the Cape Cod Canal. The
17.4-mile canal is 480 feet wide and is the world's widest sea-
level canal. Sagamore and Bourne are primarily residential areas, with year-round residents. The two bridges, the Bourne
and the Sagamore span the canal, serving as a wonderful introduction to the Cape, with panoramic vies of the canal and beyond.

On each side of the canal are bike paths, hiking trails, and
campgrounds. Enjoy a wonderful day cycling or frolic on one of
the beaches with lovely views of Cape Cod Bay.

The **Aptucxet Trading Post Museum** in Bourne includes a
Victorian Railroad Station and Herb and Wild Flower Garden.
The museum us open from May until Columbus Day.

Sagamore Beach is quite pretty and draws fewer tourists
than other beaches on the Cape.

Welcome

A Romantic Inn – Sagamore

✱ The Sea Cliff Inn

This lovely contemporary inn is located on the sea cliffs overlooking the Cape Cod Bay. The Honeymoon Suite is very romantic. It has sweeping views of the bay, a sunken two-person
Jacuzzi in the bathroom, plus many extras. The large room is
decorated in white lace and linens. Or ask for the Blue Room,
which is equally charming and decorated in country florals. It
also has wonderful views of the bay.

DONNA M. BLACKBURN

Breakfast is served either at a large dining room table or on the screened-in deck. Again, the views are spectacular. Enjoy a quiet day on the private beach below the property. On a clear day you can see Provincetown across the bay.

Innkeepers Joe and Jean Kennedy couldn't be nicer. They'll make your stay a memorable one. Open all year.

The Sea Cliff Inn
2 Indian Trail
P.O. Box 1
Sagamore Beach, MA 02562
☎ 508-888-0609

Annual Events

March

Annual Hat Parade: Sponsored by the Village Association, this Falmouth event is comprised of a parade and hat contest. Call ☎ 508-540-2585 for further details.

April

Easter Egg Hunt: There's nothing quite a fun as watching children scrambling to find chocolate Easter eggs. Sponsored by the Village Association of Falmouth, the egg hunt takes place on the lawn of the Falmouth Library. Call ☎ 508-540-2585 for information.

May

Maritime Week: This Cape-wide event includes a variety of activities, such as lighthouse tours, cruises, walking tours, and lectures. Sponsored by the Cape Cod Commission. Call ☎ 508-362-3838 for further details.

Rhododendron Festival: This Sandwich festival is an ode to the beautiful rhododendron flower, featuring a tour of the Heritage Plantation, lectures, and seed sales. Call ☎ 508-888-3300 for more information.

Falmouth-In-The-Water Boat Show: Boat enthusiasts will enjoy the display of boats at this Falmouth Harbor event. Call ☎ 508-548-2216 for further details.

June

Cape Heritage Week: The rich heritage of the Cape is celebrated throughout the region with a variety of cultural, environmental, and historical events. Call ☎ 508-888-1233 for a schedule of activities.

Annual Strawberry Festival: The Upper Cape has two separate Strawberry Festivals, one in Bourne and the other in Falmouth. The succulent fruit is given top billing in Bourne. Plan on enjoying strawberry shortcake. A free tour of the Aptucxet Trading Post is an added benefit of this event. Call ☎ 508-759-9487 for further details.

Falmouth's Festival takes place at the St. Barnabas Church with many tasty strawberry offerings. Call ☎ 508-548-8500.

Classic Car Parade: The antique cars seen at this parade on Falmouth's Main Street will capture your imagination. It all takes place on the last weekend of the month. Call ☎ 508-548-8500 for further details.

July

Fourth of July Fireworks: Celebrate Independence Day with a bang at Falmouth Heights.

Summer Garden Party: Sponsored by the Falmouth Historical Society, this event celebrates Falmouth's rich history. Refreshments and entertainment are part of the fun while you learn more about Falmouth's past. Located in a park behind the Falmouth Museum. Call ☎ 508-548-4857 for further details.

Mashpee Wampanoag Powwow: The Mashpee Wampanoag Tribal Council sponsors this powwow with Native American Indians traveling from around the country to take part in the fun. Tribal dances, Native American arts and crafts and more. Call ☎ 508-477-0208 for further details.

August

Falmouth Road Race: This annual event has been gaining popularity with runners and spectators arriving from around the world. ☎ 508-548-8500.

September

The New England Jazz Festival: Jazz enthusiasts will enjoy the beat of the music at this annual festival, which takes place at the Mashpee Commons. Call ☎ 508-477-5400 for a list of entertainers.

December

Christmas in Sandwich: You'll feel though you've turned the calendar back about a century at the Christmas in Sandwich week-long celebration. Events include Christmas caroling, B&B and museum tours and more. Sponsored by the Canal Region Chamber of Commerce. Call ☎ 508-759-6000 for further details.

Christmas By the Sea Weekend: The town of Falmouth goes all out during the first weekend in December to bring in the holiday season. Events include the lighting of thousands of Christmas lights at the Village Green, Christmas caroling at the Nobska Lighthouse, and a Christmas Parade. Call ☎ 508-548-8500 for further details.

First Night: A variety of cultural events are planned throughout the area. Call ☎ 508-790-ARTS for further details.

 Outdoor Fun

Beaches

	Admission Charge	Bath House	Beach Sticker Reqd.	Freshwater Beach	Parking Fee	Rest Rooms	Snack Bar
FALMOUTH							
Menauhant Beach,Surf Dr.					*	*	*
Old Silver Beach, W. Falmouth		*			*	*	*
Surf Drive Beach,Surf Dr.		*			*	*	*
MASHPEE							
Hathaway's Pond	*			*		*	
John's Pond Park, Off Hoophole Rd.			*		*	*	
South Cape Beach, Great Oak Rd.					*	*	
BOURNE							
Monument Beach, Off Rte. 28						*	*
SANDWICH							
East Sandwich Beach, N. Shore Blvd.	*						
Scusset Beach, At Rtes. 6 and 3	*	*				*	*
Town Neck Beach, Off Rte. 6A	*						
Wakeby Beach, John Ewer Rd.	*						

Within its 68 miles of coastline, there are many beaches in and around the **Falmouth area**, situated on either Buzzards Bay and Vineyard Sound. The water has an average summer temperature of 70°. The beaches are sandy and have relatively mild surf.

Many of the beaches require a parking sticker showing proof of residency. If you are staying in the area for more than a week, and have proof of residency such as a rental agreement, you can purchase a pass at the **Surf Drive Bath House**, ☎ 508-548-8623. Your innkeeper may also have guest beach passes available. At the public beaches, you may purchase a parking pass for the day.

Forests, Preserves & Parks

In Woods Hole

Peaceful **Quissett Harbor** has several pleasant walking trails and a path leading to the Knob, which offers spectacular views of Buzzards Bay. A perfect place for a walk at sunset. Take a peaceful stroll through the waterfront garden.

Spohr's Garden (on Fells Road) is known for its display of spring daffodils and summer flowers.

In Falmouth

Enjoy 387 acres of conservation woodland with marked trails at **Beebe Woods**, located off Ter Huen Drive. The **Ashumet Holly Reservations** here offers lectures, guided tours, seal cruises, and island tours. There are 45 acres of marked trails through holly and franklinia preserve.

There are 1,600 acres of woodlands for hiking, birdwatching, and horseback riding at the **Frances Crane Wildlife Management** (off Highway 151).

Experience farming as it once was at the historic **Bourne Farm**. Enjoy the farm's 34 acres of hiking trails through orchards and woodlands overlooking Crocker Pond. In the fall, the farm hosts the Pumpkin Day Festival. Call the Nature Center, ☎ 508-564-6262, for hours and scheduled events.

The **Waquoit Bay National Esturine Research Reserve's** 2,500 acres is New England coastline at its best. Trek by open waters, barriers beaches, and marshes. The reserve includes Washburn Island and South Cape Beach State Park. Located on Route 28. Call ☎ 508-457-0495 for more information.

Between Sagamore & Sandwich

The **Scusset Beach Reservation** covers 490 acres and offers hiking, biking and picnicking, plus a beach and camping opportunities. Located near the Cape Cod Canal on Scusset Road, off Route 3. Call ☎ 508-888-0859 for further details.

The **Shawme-Crowell State Forest** has 742 acres of forests for outdoor fun in the sun. Located off Route 130 in Sandwich, call ☎ 508-888-0351.

THE CAPE COD CANAL REGION: The Army Corps of Engineers sponsors a variety of activities, including guided walking tours, and hiking and bicycling opportunities. Stop at the visitor center for information. A picnic area outside the center affords wonderful views of the canal. Located on the mainland side of the canal, on Route 6 in Bournesdale. Call ☎ 508-759-4431.

Recreation

Golf

The following clubs all offer 18-hole courses.

Ballymeade Country Club, 125 Falmouth Woods Drive, Rt. 151, North Falmouth, ☎ 508-540-4005.

Cape Cod Country Club, on Theater Drive in North Falmouth. ☎ 508-563-9842.

Falmouth Country Club, 630 Carriage Shop Road, Falmouth. ☎ 508-548-3211.

Harney Paul Golf Club, 74 Club Valley Drive in East Falmouth. ☎ 508-563-3454.

Quashnet Valley Country Club, 309 Old Barnstable Road, Mashpee, ☎ 508-477-4412.

Tennis

Most of the clubs below don't have telephones. Simply stop by to book a court.

North Falmouth, Nye Park

West Falmouth, Blacksmith Road (behind the fire station)

East Falmouth, Elementary School, Davisville Road

Woods Hole, Bell Tower

Lawrence School, Lakeview Avenue, Falmouth

Falmouth High School, Gifford Street Exit, Falmouth (☎ 508-457-2567).

Falmouth Sports Center (indoors and outdoors), Highfield Drive, Falmouth (☎ 508-548-7433).

Bicycling

The Falmouth and Woods Hole residents are very proud of their **Shining Sea Trail Bike Path**. It's a 3.3-mile bike path that leads past forests and along coastline. There's a beach along the way, so bring your swimsuit. The trail begins on Locust Street in Falmouth and ends at the ferry terminal in Woods Hole. There is an access point at Elm Road. For travel to both north and east Falmouth locations, access is at Oyster Pond. The eastern route follows the coast from Falmouth Beach to Menahunt Beach. The western route will take you past Quisett, Sippewisett, West Falmouth and Old Silver Beach.

On either side of the **Cape Cod Canal** are bicycle paths. There are 6½ miles of bike trails on the south side and eight miles on the north side. Take time off the bicycle to appreciate a view of the Bourne and Sagamore bridges and the comings and going of canal vessels.

Cruises/Ferries/Sailing

The *Island Queen* (to Oak Bluffs). Falmouth Heights Road, Falmouth, ☎ 508-548-4800.

Falmouth-Edgartown Ferry, 278 Scranton Avenue, Falmouth, ☎ 508-548-9400

Woods Hole Steamship Authority, Railroad Avenue, Woods Hole ☎ 508-477-8600

Cape Cod Windsurfing Academy, 134 Menauhant Road, Falmouth Heights, ☎ 508-495-0008.

Patriot Party Boats, 227 Clinton Ave, Falmouth, ☎ 508-548-2626 or 800-734-0088.

Sailing lessons are offered through the **Falmouth Recreation Department**, and the **Falmouth Yacht Club**; windsurfing lessons are also available. Call ☎ 508-548-8500.

The Upper Cape

Marine Facilities / Public Landings

For further information regarding marinas in this areas, call the **Harbor Master** at ☎ 508-457-2550. The following offer transient slips, gas, diesel and other boating supplies: Falmouth Inner Harbor; Green Pond/Harbor; Woods Hole, Eel Pond; Fiddlers Cove.

Entertainment

Movies

Falmouth Mall Cinema (fourplex), Falmouth Mall, Teaticket, ☎ 508-540-2169.

Theater

Several professional theaters in Falmouth offer a variety of entertainment, including Broadway productions, classics, musicals, comedies, and dramas.

The **Highfield Summer Theater** hosts the College Light Opera Company. It's off Depot Avenue, ☎ 508-548-0668.

Theatre on the Bay, trading Post Corners, Monument Beach, ☎ 508-759-0977. Produces eight plays per season, four of which are written by local playwrights.

Highfield Theatre, off Depot Avenue, Falmouth, ☎ 508-548-0668.

College Light Opera Company, off Depot Avenue, Falmouth, ☎ 508-548-0668.

Tours

Falmouth Tour Company, Falmouth, ☎ 508-548-4100.

Seaside Tours, ☎ 508-495-0035.

Treasure Hunt Enterprises, West Falmouth, ☎ 508-540-1795.

Reaching The Upper Cape

By Car

From New York: Take I-95 through Connecticut and Rhode Island. From Providence, take I-195 East. At Bourne, take Route 25 East (I-195 South) over Bourne Bridge, to Route 28 South.

From Boston: Take Route 3 to the Sagamore Bridge, then follow Route 6 West to Route 28 South. Or follow I-95 to Route 24 and take I-495 to Buzzards Bay (Bourne). Cross the Bourne Bridge to Route 28 South.

By Air

The closest airport for commercial flights is **Hyannis**, which is about 20 miles from Falmouth. Airlines serving this area are: **Cape Air**, with service from Boston to Hyannis, ☎ 800-352-0714; and **US Air Express**, with service to Hyannis from Nantucket and New York and seasonal service from Washington, D.C., ☎ 800-352-0714.

By Bus

Bonanza Bus, ☎ 800-556-3815. Daily service from Logan Airport and South Station in Boston, and from New York City and Providence to Falmouth and Woods Hole.

The Upper Cape

For More Information

Cape Cod Chamber of Commerce, ☎ 508-759-6000.

Falmouth Chamber of Commerce, ☎ 508-548-8500.

Sandwich Chamber of Commerce, ☎ 508-759-6000.

The Mid-Cape

The Mid-Cape is a mixed bag. Water views here are stupendous, including sites along beautiful Nantucket Sound to the south and Cape Cod Bay to the north. However, the center part of the Mid-Cape has been lost to 20th-century America with strip malls and all the trappings of modern society. My suggestion is to stay as close to the water as possible.

The three towns comprising the Mid-Cape are Barnstable, Dennis, and Yarmouth. Within each town are villages. My favorite part of the Mid-Cape is along Route 6A (also known as Old King's Highway). It's by far one of the loveliest routes in our country. Here you will find a host of beautiful inns, old Colonial-style homes, and country lanes. The pretty beaches lining Cape Cod Bay are perfect for exploring the seashore, swimming and sunbathing.

DONNA M. BLACKBURN

Barnstable/Hyannis

Barnstable is comprised of seven different villages – Centerville, Osterville, Cotuit, Marstons Mills, Hyannis, Barnstable Village, and West Barnstable. Each village has its own distinct flavor. The largest village is Hyannis, really a small city unto itself. Near Hyannis is Hyannisport, famous for its connection to the Kennedy family. West Barnstable and Barnstable Village on Route 6A and Osterville and Cotuit on Nantucket Sound are the least spoiled areas.

Romantic Hotels & Inns

🎋 The Crocker Tavern Bed and Breakfast

Innkeepers Jeff and Sue Carlson should be commended for their wonderful restoration of The Crocker Tavern Bed and Breakfast. Originally a stagecoach stop, the circa 1754 home has retained much of its Georgian Colonial charm.

All of the five guest rooms are romantic. I particularly liked the Julia Crocker Room, with its working fireplace, carved poster canopied queen bed and antique Empire dresser. Soft pink, blues, and whites give the room an airy quality. I also enjoyed Aunt Lydia's Room, which has a queen-size Shaker bed, working fireplace, and antique furnishings.

Candlelight and soft music set the atmosphere for the hearty continental breakfast. The table is set with Blue Danube china and lead crystal glasses. A breakfast for champions! There are two gardens on the property, perfect places to read a book or just plain relax.

Crocker Tavern Bed and Breakfast
3095 Olde Kings Highway
Barnstable, MA 02630

☎ *508-362-5115 or 800-773-5359*
Fax 508-362-5562
E-mail crocktav@capecod.net
www.capecod.net/crockertavernbnb
$$$

❦ The Ackworth Inn

The Ackworth has lots of wonderful light. The cheerful blend of
antique and country furnishings gives it a romantic feel all of
its own. Each of the six rooms has a unique quality. The Cum-
maquid Room is an elegant first-floor room with double French
doors, fireplace, and antique double bed. The old-fashioned
English wallpaper in the Chatham Room gives a whimsical ef-
fect. Or consider the bright and sunny Orleans Room, located
on the first floor of the carriage house.

DONNA M. BLACKBURN

The Ackworth's nightly turn-down service includes a tasty
chocolate treat and a miniature rose. A full breakfast is served
in the country-style kitchen or on the deck overlooking the back
yard. Most of the fresh fruits and vegetables served for break-

fast are grown in the garden. This inn is a real treat! Open year-round.

The Ackworth Inn
4352 Old King's Highway, P.O. Box 256
Cummaquid, MA 02637
☎ *800-362-6363 or 508-362-3330*
$$$

✦ The Beechwood Inn

The Beechwood Inn has seen more than its share of marriage proposals, anniversary celebrations, and romantic interludes. The inn is a carefully restored Queen-Anne home with many romantic touches. There are six guest rooms. Sweethearts will enjoy the Eastlake Room with its William Morris wallpaper, spoon carved bed, and matching marble topped dresser. The room looks out at Cape Cod Bay through colored glass windows. The Garret Room has a wonderful cozy attic quality. The

DONNA M. BLACKBURN

angled walls give the room its hideaway feel, as does the period paneling and an 1850s brass bed. A panoramic view of Cape Cod Bay can be seen from the Palladian window.

A full gourmet breakfast is served daily in the old-fashioned dining room. Enjoy an afternoon tea while sitting on the veranda, overlooking an acre of flowers, trees, and shrubs. Innkeepers Debbie and Ken Traugot couldn't be friendlier.

The Beechwood Inn
2839 Main Street, Route 6A
Barnstable, MA 02630
☎ 508-362-6618; Fax 508-362-0298 or 800-609-6618
E-mail bwdinn@virtualcapecod.com
www.virtualcapecod.com / market / beechwood /
$$$

❦ The Inn at Fernbrook

The Inn at Fernbrook is located on an estate originally landscaped by Frederick Law Olmsted, famous for his designing of Boston's Emerald Necklace and New York's Central Park. The grounds here are breathtaking. The heart-shaped rose garden was designed with romantics in mind; a duck pond is also on

DONNA M. BLACKBURN

The Mid-Cape

the property. The 1881 Queen Anne home is majestic, featuring seven guest rooms all decorated with period antiques. Enjoy the privacy of the Garden Cottage, tucked away in the garden. The Olmsted Suite has a vaulted ceiling in the bedroom, a working fireplace in the living room, and its own roof deck. This is one of the Cape's most romantic places to stay. Open throughout the year.

The Inn at Fernbrook
481 Main Street
Centerville, MA 02632
☎ 508-775-4334
Fax 508-778-4455
$$$

The Ashley Manor

There's something quite grand about entering the Ashley Manor estate. Hidden behind a huge privet hedge, the Manor is wonderfully secluded. Romantics will enjoy the privacy of the Garden Cottage Suite, with its queen-size bed, fireplace, private whirlpool, and terrace. The Terrace Room is also a cozy nesting place for lovers. It has a brass bed, wicker furniture, fireplace, and private terrace.

The spacious parlor and library are carefully appointed with period antiques, oriental rugs, and country furnishings. Enjoy a full gourmet breakfast in the formal dining room or on the deck overlooking the garden. The lovely grounds are reminiscent of an English manor and include spacious lawns, a gazebo and, for tennis enthusiasts, an all-weather regulation tennis court.

Ashley Manor
Box 856
Olde Kings Highway
Barnstable, MA 02630
☎ 508-362-8044 or 888-535-2246
Fax 508-362-9927
www.capecod.net/ashleymn
E-mail ashleymn@capecod.net
$$$

Honeysuckle Hill

This small and intimate inn has a country feel to it. Decorated in blues and whites, the dining room and sitting room areas are inviting. The guest rooms are equally charming. My favorite was room five, which has a separate entrance up a flight of stairs. The room is furnished with antiques from the innkeeper's grandmother's collection. The grounds are quite pretty. Play a game of crochet or read a book under one of the trees.

A full breakfast is served daily. Homemade lemonade is offered as an afternoon treat.

Honeysuckle Hill
591 Main Street
West Barnstable, MA 02668
☎ 508-362-8418 or 800-441-8418
Fax 508-362-4914
$$$

Restaurants

Alberto's Ristorante

This well-received Italian restaurant on Hyannis' Main Street offers homemade pasta dishes and a variety of chicken, seafood, and lamb entrées. The menu is extensive, the decor is intimate and elegant. What more could you ask for?

Alberto's Restaurant
360 Main Street
Hyannis
☎ 508-778-1770
$$$

The Mid-Cape

The Roadhouse Café

The Roadhouse Café features Italian and American cuisine and offers a rather extensive menu. The softly lit dining room is intimate, with a dark wood-beam ceiling; the tables are draped in white linen and set with candles. Outdoor seating is available during the summer.

The Roadhouse Café
488 South Street
Hyannis
☎ 508-775-2386
Fax 508-778-1025
$$$

The Paddock

Here's a chance to play word association. Ask anyone to name the best restaurant in the Mid-Cape and "The Paddock" will be their answer. Located next to the Melody Tent, it offers a first-rate dining experience. The decor offers up a Victorian elegance. Candlelight and fresh-cut flowers adorn linen-covered tables. Menu selections feature a variety of seafood, poultry, and beef dishes. This is a perfect place to dine before catching a concert next door.

The Paddock
West End Rotary
Hyannis
☎ 508-775-7677
$$$

The Black Cat

Overlooking Hyannis Harbor, this popular restaurant offers seafood and pasta lunch and dinner dishes and a scrumptious Sunday brunch. The decor follows a maritime theme and has a huge model ship and saltwater aquarium. Outdoor seating is available, weather willing.

The Black Cat
165 Ocean Street
Hyannis
☎ *508-778-1233*
$$$

Cape Cod Dinner Train

You probably are too young to remember the days when trains were the main way to travel and when the food served on the train was part of the whole experience. The Cape Cod Dinner Train will take you back to the days of yore. Tables are set with white linen and a single red rose. Classical music plays quietly in the background. The menu is varied, with seafood, meat, and vegetarian dishes available. Boarding the train in Hyannis, you'll enjoy a 40-mile, three-hour tour of the Mid-Cape and portions of Sandwich and the Cape Cod Canal.

The Cape Cod Dinner Train
Main Street
Hyannis
☎ *508-771-3788*
$$$$

The Regatta of Cotuit

Fine dining in an intimate atmosphere is the trademark of The Regatta of Cotuit. Picture an 18th-century inn with eight small dining rooms. Candles light the tables and soft piano music plays in the background. Menu entrées are imaginative, with such selections as sea scallops caramelized in a spicy ginger oil with Asian greens, citrus glaze and plantain chips, or boneless loin of lamb with spinach, pinenuts and Vermont chevre, encased in pastry.

The Regatta of Cotuit
Route 28
Cotuit
☎ *508-428-5715*
$$$$

The Mid-Cape

Touring
Barnstable/Hyannis

The best of the Mid-Cape is on Old King's Highway, also known as Route 6A. Here you will find long stretches of beautiful homes, cozy bed and breakfasts and an assortment of antique shops, restaurants, and more.

Barnstable was established in 1639, two years after Sandwich, making it the second-oldest town in the area. Barnstable is comprised of a number of villages. Barnstable Village is situated on Old King's Highway and is considered the county seat. The **Olde Colonial Courthouse**, located on Route 6A, was built in 1772 and is the second-oldest courthouse in the United States. The Tale of Cape Cod, a local group dedicated to preserving the Cape's history, sponsors a series of lectures/slide shows here during the summer months. Call ☎ 508-362-8927 for further information.

The **Sturgis Library** holds the distinction of being the oldest library in the United States. A portion of it was built in 1644; in 1867 the library was extended. The library is currently known for its interesting collection of Cape genealogical and maritime history. Located on Route 6A. Call ☎ 508-362-6636 for further details.

The **Trayser Museum Complex** has a number of exhibits and offerings. The red-painted brick building, located on 6A, houses maritime and Indian artifacts, ship models, and Sandwich glass. The building's downstairs has been recreated to look like it did in the mid-18th century when the building operated as a Customs House. Also on the grounds is a jail, complete with inmates' graffiti. The jail dates back to 1690.

Hyannis is by far the busiest town on the Cape (ironic, since it is called a "village" here on the Cape). Portions of Hyannis are quite charming. Main Street has a certain old-fashioned city-center feel to it and the port is quite active and colorful. Unfortunately, Hyannis' center has enough strip malls to discourage visitors from enjoying its finer points.

Hyannis' connection with the Kennedy family spans many years. In nearby Hyannisport, the **Kennedy Compound** was the summer White House during the Kennedy administration and continues to be where the Kennedys come to vacation. The compound is best seen by taking one of the harbor tours that sails by it.

Other acknowledgements of JFK's contribution to our country include the **John F. Kennedy Memorial** and the **John F. Kennedy Hyannis Museum**. The John F. Kennedy Memorial is located next to Veteran's Park and overlooks Lewis Bay. A fountain pool was built in his memory by the people of Barnstable in 1966. The John F. Kennedy Hyannis Museum is located in Main Street's Old Town Hall. Kennedy's life is told through annotated photographs, with special emphasis on the years he spent in Cape Cod. Located at 397 Main Street, the museum is open daily throughout the summer. Call ☎ 508-775-2201 for more information.

The **Melody Tent** has been a long-time entertainment center for the Cape featuring a number of first-rate performers. Located on West Main Street. Call ☎ 508-775-9100 for further details.

The **Cape Cod Scenic Railroad** offers an opportunity to see portions of the Cape that can't be viewed by car. The train ride will take you to Sandwich, past cranberry bogs, salt marshes, and other Cape Cod terrain. You can board the train at the Downtown Hyannis Station at Main and Center Streets. Call ☎ 508-771-3788 for scheduling and fare information.

Osterville is exactly how I envisioned the Cape before I ever lived here. Nineteenth-century seaside houses dot the landscape. Sailboats glide over the water of Nantucket Sound. The water catches the light from the sun and glitters while sea grass moves gently with the wind. Nearby a pleasant downtown area offers an array of boutiques, gift shops, and restaurants.

Visit the **1856 Country Store**, formerly referred to as a penny-candy store. Prices have changed, but the store's general atmosphere has remained the same. The store is located at 555 Main Street.

A collection of antiques dolls and furnishings are exhibited at the **Osterville Historical Society Museum**, 155 West Bay Road. Next door are the **Boat Shop Museum** and the 18th-century **Cammett House**. Call ☎ 508-428-5861 for further details.

In **Centerville**, you'll be delighted by the sea captain homes which line quiet tree-shaded streets. The popular **Craigville Beach**, known for its long stretch of protected ocean beach on Nantucket Sound, is located here. Take a moment to catch the panoramic view at **Shoot Flying Hill Road**, the highest point of land on the Cape.

Centerville Historical Society Museum has a variety of exhibits, including furnished period rooms and Sandwich glass and maritime artifacts. Of particular note is the museum's collection of miniature bird carvings by Anthony Elmer Crowell. Also interesting is the museum's exhibit of 300 quilts and costumes, spanning three centuries. Located at 513 Main Street, call ☎ 508-775-0331 for more information.

DONNA M. BLACKBURN

Yarmouth & Yarmouth Port

As with the rest of the Mid-Cape, Yarmouth extends from Cape Cod Bay to Nantucket Sound. Yarmouth Port follows the Old King's Highway and is by far the prettiest part of the area.

Welcome

Romantic Inns & Hotels

☘ Liberty Hill Inn

The Liberty Hill Inn offers a perfect blend of elegance and style. As you enter the three-story main house, you'll enjoy the spacious living and dining rooms with their tall floor-to-ceiling windows and light-colored walls.

Honeymooners will enjoy the Waterford Suite, decorated in a subtle grey-and-white theme. It has a king-size bed and a view of the bay. Also for the romantic is the Cranberry Room, with its queen-size canopy bed, floral wallpaper, and white linens. I particularly like Liberty Hill's newest addition, the four guest rooms situated in the Carriage House. Built in 1825, the Carriage House was transformed in 1997 to include these large, lovely rooms with exposed ceiling beams and corner fireplaces. Two of the rooms in the Carriage House have private whirlpools. The Carriage House is a testament to blending the old and new. A full breakfast is served daily in the dining room. Open year-round.

> *The Liberty Hill*
> *77 Main Street*
> *Yarmouth Port, MA 02675*
> ☎ *800-821-3977 or 508-362-3976*
> *Fax 508-362-6485*
> *www.sunsol.com / libertyhillinn*
> *E-mail libertyh@capecod.net*
> *$$$*

The Mid-Cape

❦ The Inn at Cape Cod

There's something stately about this Greek Revival inn. The exterior has two-story columns. Inside, 10 guests rooms are decorated with antiques and period reproductions. Ascend a grand staircase to the second floor, where you will find the Village Suite. It features a hand-carved mahogany queen-size bed, Italian armoire, floor-to-ceiling windows, sitting room, and private balcony. Downstairs is the Joshua Sears Room, with wonderful floor-to-ceiling windows and a four-poster mahogany bed. A full breakfast buffet and afternoon tea are served daily. Open year-round.

D.M. BLACKBURN

The Inn at Cape Cod
4 Summer Street, P.O. Box 96
Yarmouth Port, MA 02675
☎ 800-850-7301 or 508-375-0590
www.capecod.com / inn-at-capecod
$$$

✈ The Wedgewood Inn

The three-story Wedgewood Inn has an elegant feel to it. Each room is decorated with hand-crafted cherrywood pencil-post beds, antique quilts, and period wallpapering. Many of the rooms have working fireplaces. Romantics will enjoy the Deluxe Suite, which features a fireplace, separate sitting room, and furnished screened-in porch. The entire third floor is one suite with its own separate sitting room. The recently renovated Carriage Barn offers three distinctive suites with fireplaces and private decks.

DONNA M. BLACKBURN

The inn serves a full breakfast and an afternoon tea daily. Open year-round.

The Wedgewood Inn
83 Main Street
Yarmouth Port, MA 02675
☎ *508-362-9178 or 508-362-5157*
Fax 508-362-5851
www.virtualcapecod.com / market / wedgewoodinn
$$$

Restaurants

Abbicci

Striking decor and innovative Italian food define Abbicci. The colorful interior and the black slate bar give the restaurant its contemporary feel. Menu selections include native seafood, pastas, and meat dishes. A favorite dining spot in the Mid-Cape, reservations are recommended. Open for lunch and dinner; a Sunday brunch has also been well received.

> *Abbicci*
> *43 Main Street (Route 6A)*
> *Yarmouth Port*
> ☎ *508-362-3501*

Inaho

The Cape's one and only Japanese restaurant, Inaho has been generating a reputation for its tasty dishes. Fresh, local seafood is the prime ingredient. Sushi, tempura, teriyaki, and sashimi are all served here. A beautiful Japanese garden is located behind the restaurant. Opened for dinner, year-round.

> *Inaho*
> *157 Route 6A*
> *Yarmouth Port*
> ☎ *508-362-5522*
> *$$$*

DONNA M. BLACKBURN

Jack's Outback

For a good time, call Jack's Outback, where the fun-loving staff will give you a bad time and you'll beg for more! I look forward to the day when a situation comedy is based on this restaurant. Take note of the welcome mat reading "Go Away." The handwritten menu is comprised of local seafood favorites. There's no romance here, but you'll still have a great time.

Jack's Outback
161 Main Street
Yarmouth Port
☎ *508-362-6690*
$$

Hallet's Store

This 1889 drugstore serves lunch counter food items, sandwiches, fries, frappes, and ice-cream sodas. The ambiance is pure 19th-century with an all-marble soda fountain and swivel stools.

Hallet's Store
139 Route 6A
Yarmouth Port
☎ *508-362-3362*
$

Touring Yarmouth Port

The Indian name for Yarmouth is Mattachesse, meaning the "planting lands." Settled in 1639 by farmers from the Plymouth Bay Company, Yarmouth Port was incorporated in 1829. Like the rest of the region, it was transformed from a farming area to a maritime community over the past centuries.

Yarmouth Port's history is chronicalled in the old photographs and memorabilia displayed at the **Taylor Hallet Museum**. Call ☎ 508-362-3362 for more information.

The **Winslow Crocker House** has an interesting history. Built in West Barnstable in 1847, this two-story Georgian was split down the middle and divided by the sons of Winslow Crocker upon his death. In 1936, Mary Thatcher bought the home and moved it to its present location. She donated the house and collection of 17th-, 18th-, 19th-century furniture to the Society for the Preservation of New England Antiquities. Take note of the home's 12-over-12 small pane windows and wood paneling. Located at 250 Route 6A. Call ☎ 508-362-4385 for further details.

Also of historical significance is **Captain Bangs Hallet House**, at 11 Strawberry Lane. The original part of this Greek Revival house was built in 1740. A century later, additional portions of the house were built. The kitchen has its original 1740 brick beehive oven and butter churn. A nice collection of china, pewter, maritime artifacts, and clothing from the sea captain era are displayed here. Open throughout the summer on select afternoons. Call ☎ 508-362-3021 for further details.

Picnic tables and walking trails offer you the chance to spend a leisurely afternoon at the **Taylor-Bray Farm**, located on Bray Farm Road. The farm was established in the late 1700s. It continues to be a working farm and is listed on the National Register of Historical Places. Open throughout the summer, call ☎ 508-398-2231, ext. 292 for more information.

Once the site of a schooner shipyard, the **Bass Hole Boardwalk** will take you past marshlands to Gray's Beach. At the end of the boardwalk are benches overlooking Dennis's Chapin Beach. The **Botanical Trails of the Historical Society of Old Yarmouth** also offer outdoor splendor with 50 acres of oak and pine woods, berry plants, rhododendrons and other Cape flora. Located behind the post office on Route 6A, the trails are open throughout the year during daylight hours.

Dennis

Dennis extends from Nantucket Sound to Cape Cod Bay. The northern portions of Dennis, following the Old King's Highway, offer visitors the chance to explore a town relatively untouched by the 20th century. Here you will find many sea captain homes transformed into museums and inns. A thriving cranberry industry began in Dennis in the early 1800s and continues to be part of the Dennis experience. Outdoor opportunities include several conservation areas and nature trails. The Cape Cod Rail Trail (one of the Cape's most popular bike paths) originates in Dennis, extending 20 miles east to Eastham.

Romantic Inns

Isaiah Hall Bed and Breakfast Inn

Far away from the crowds, this 1857 farmhouse, located on a country lane, offers a perfect respite. The country motif is wonderfully executed in the common rooms and 10 guest quarters. Among my favorites is Room One, with its blue, green, and white floral decorations, a crocheted canopy bed, and fireplace. Room Ten has slanted ceilings and a cottage turn-of-the-century bed. A two-story gathering room in the Carriage House is quite homey, the perfect place to meet other travelers. Breakfast is served in dining room on a 12-foot cherry table. Open mid-April through mid-October.

The Isaiah Hall B&B Inn
152 Whig Street
P.O. Box 1007
Dennis, MA 02638
☎ 508-385-9928 or 800-736-0160
Fax 508-385-5879
E-mail isaiah@capecod.net
Web page: www.virtualcapecod.com / market / isaiahhall /
$$$

The Four Chimneys Inn

This circa 1857 Victorian home has maintained its elegance through the years. The common rooms on the first floor include a living room, dining room, and library, each with a marble fireplace. A beautiful freestanding staircase leads you upstairs. Here you will find eight charming guest rooms. The Strawberry Suite has a separate sitting room and private deck. The Teaberry Room is quite pretty, featuring an antique oak queen-size bed, decorative marble fireplace, and a view of the woods through French doors. On the third floor are several additional guest quarters, many with stenciled walls. Enjoy breakfast on the screened-in porch overlooking the extensive perennial gardens.

> *The Four Chimneys Inn*
> *946 Main Street*
> *Route 6A*
> *Dennis, MA 02638*
> ☎ *508-385-6317*
> *$$$*

✦ The Scargo Manor Bed and Breakfast

This is one of my favorite bed and breakfasts on the Cape. It's a beautifully restored 1895 sea captain's home situated on Scargo Lake. The Captain Howes Suite is a two-room suite with a king-size canopy bed and an attached sitting room with a queen-size sofabed and fireplace. Across the hall is the Prin-

DONNA M. BLACKBURN

cess Scargo Suite, which offers a queen-size canopy bed and separate sitting room with views of Scargo Lake.

An extended continental breakfast is served daily in the formal dining room or on the enclosed porch during summer months.

Scargo Manor Bed and Breakfast
909 Main Street
Route 6A
Dennis, MA 02638
☎ *800-595-0034 or 508-385-5534*
Web page: www.virtualcapecod.com / market / scargomanor
$$$

Restaurants

The Red Pheasant

Housed in a restored 200-year-old barn and considered one of the Cape's premiere restaurants, the Red Pheasant couldn't be more romantic. The cozy interior encourages intimacy. Food selections include such entrées as pan-roasted salmon with ginger, shallots, pink peppercorns, and shiitake mushrooms finished with white wine and cream. Or consider the hazelnut-crusted Statler chicken with chèvre, pumpernickel croutons, and a sherry and hazelnut vinagrette.

The Red Pheasant
905 Route 6A
Dennis
☎ *508-385-2133*
$$$$

Gina's By The Sea

Gina's By The Sea celebrated its 50th birthday in 1998 and has been a long-time Mid-Cape favorite. The dining room overlooks the bay, and a fireplace and knotty pine paneling add to the at-

The Mid-Cape

mosphere. The cuisine is Northern Italian, with a variety of seafood and pasta dishes. Open for lunch and dinner throughout the summer months.

Gina's By The Sea
134 Taunton Avenue
Dennis
☎ *508-385-3213*
$$$

Scargo Café

Located next to the Cape Playhouse, the Scargo Café offers Italian cuisine until midnight during the summer months. Its atrium and greenhouse dining rooms are intimate. Consider capelli d'angelo, touted a feast of angel hair pasta with a touch of proscuitto ham in a rich tomato and garlic cream sauce, or grilled lamb loin with mint jelly.

The Scargo Café
799 Main Street
Dennis
☎ *508-385-8200*
Fax ☎ *508-385-6977*
$$

The Green Room Restaurant

Sister to the Scargo Café, the Green Room Restaurant is all light and air under a cathedral ceiling. The eclectic menu includes fresh seafood and vegetables with a Creole influence. Located on the grounds of the Cape Playhouse, it's a good choice for a pre-theater meal.

The Green Room Restaurant
36 Hope Lane, off Route 6A
Dennis
☎ *508-385-8000*
$$

Touring Dennis

Much like its surrounding towns, Dennis began as a farming community, later became a town for seafaring captains and then branched out into the cranberry-growing and salt-making industries. At the height of the whaling days, over 300 sea captains lived in Dennis.

Dennis is home of the **Cape Playhouse**, one of the oldest theaters in the United States. Featuring Broadway shows and children's theater, the playhouse is an Equity Theatre. Famous actors such as Gregory Peck and Henry Fonda have performed here. Located on Main Street on Route 6A. Call ☎ 508-385-3911 for their schedule. Also on the Playhouse grounds is the **Cape Museum of Fine Arts**. Over 500 pieces of art comprise the permanent collection, featuring famous Cape Cod artists. The museum sponsors a classic film series, lectures, art classes, and trips. ☎ 508-385-4477. Romantics will enjoy the view from **Scargo Hill**, where you can see the lake glisten. A historical marker tells the tower's history and points out sights. On a clear day you'll glimpses of Provincetown in the distance.

Indian Legends

A local Indian legend tells the story of Princess Scargo of the Nobscusset Tribe. The princess was loved by an Indian brave who had to leave his tribe on a trip. He gave her four fish to take care of while he was away. It was a summer with little rain and the ponds had already dried up. Her father, the tribal Chief, asked the women and children to dig a pond for the fish. Princess Scargo's tears filled the pond and the fish were able to stay alive.

Annual Events

February

President's Day Antique Show and Sale in Hyannis is held on the third weekend in February. The event takes place at the Cape Codder Hotel on Route 132. Call ☎ 508-775-2280.

April

Osterville's **Daff O'Ville Days** pay homage to the flower and include an antique car show, music and a fashion show. Call ☎ 508-428-6327.

May

Maritime Week is celebrated Cape-wide and includes lighthouse tours, open house tours, walks, and lectures. Call ☎ 508-362-3838.

The **Annual Waterfront Festival** is held in Hyannis on the second weekend in May. Here you will be able to view the works of 100 artists and craftmakers. Call ☎ 800-4HYANNIS.

The Memorial Day weekend **Figawi Sailboat Race** is a much talked about sailboat race from Hyannis to Nantucket. Call ☎ 800-4HYANNIS.

June

Cape Heritage Week takes place throughout the Cape and features a variety of historical walks, tours, and events. Call ☎ 508-888-1233.

July

Don't miss the fireworks in Hyannis on **Independence Day**.

The **Barnstable County Fair** has been taking place for over a century. There's something for everyone: rides, food booths, livestock shows, art shows, and baked goods contests. Located at the Barnstable Fair Grounds on Route 151. Call ☎ 508-563-3200.

The Cape Cod Symphony Summer Concert takes place at the Hyannis Town Green on the first Saturday of the month. Call ☎ 800-4HYANNIS.

August

The Centerville Library sponsors **Centerville Old Home Week** with a number of fun activities scheduled in mid-August. An ice-cream social, tea party, and outdoor country line dance party are all part of the fun. Call ☎ 508-775-1787.

Jazz By The Sea is a popular Hyannis event taking place on the Hyannis Town Green. Call ☎ 800-4HYANNIS.

Pops By the Sea also happens in Hyannis, usually on the first Sunday of the month. Call ☎ 508-790-2787.

The **West Barnstable Village Festival** includes an antique auto show, children's activities, food booths and more. Call ☎ 508-362-3225.

The **Annual Dennis Festival Days** are celebrated in a week-long festival which offers sandcastle-building and kite-flying contests, an antique car parade, hayrides, farm tours, an arts and crafts show and more. Call ☎ 508-398-3568.

The Mid-Cape

October

The **Yarmouth Seaside Festival** takes place on the second weekend in October. This event includes a parade, live music, children's activities, various races and competitions, and a fireworks display at night. Call ☎ 508-778-1008.

December

Christmas Strolls take place throughout the Mid-Cape area, including the Barnstable Village Christmas Stroll, the Centerville Village Christmas Stroll, and the Yarmouth Port Christmas Stroll.

Osterville Village also sponsors a **Christmas Open House** event.

The **Hyannis Christmas Harbor Lighting** brings a boat parade, harbor tours, and the lighting of the Village Green. Santa is destined to pop up in various locations during the week-long event. Call ☎ 800-4HYANNIS.

First Night is a Cape-Wide event, bringing in the New Year with lots of music, dance, and cultural events. Call ☎ 508-790-ARTS.

 # Outdoor Fun

Beaches

Use the following chart to determine which beach best suits your needs.

	Admission Charge	Bath House	Beach Sticker Reqd.	Freshwater Beach	Parking Fee	Rest Rooms	Snack Bar
DENNIS							
Chapin Memorial Beach, Off Rte. 6A	*				*	*	
Corporation Road Beach, Off Rte. 6A	*	*			*	*	*
Glendon Road Beach, Off Rte. 28	*				*	*	
Haigis Beach, Off Rte. 28	*				*	*	
Horsefoot Path Beach, Off Rte. 6A	*						
Howes Street Beach, Off Rte. 6A	*				*		
Inman Road Beach, Chase Ave.	*				*	*	
Mayflower Beach, Off Rte. 6A	*				*	*	*
Princess Beach, OffScargo Hill Road	*			*	*	*	
Raycroft Parking Beach, Old Wharf Rd	*				*		
Scargo Lake, Off Rte. 6A	*			*	*	*	
Sea Street Beach, Off Rte. 6A	*				*	*	
Sea Street Beach, Sea St. & Old Wharf Road	*				*	*	
South Village Rd. Beach, Off Lower County	*				*	*	
West Dennis Beach, Off Rte. 28	*	*			*	*	*
HARWICH							
Red River Beach, Off Rte.28					*		*
CHATHAM							
Cockle Cove Beach, Off Rte. 28					*	*	
Hardings Beach, Off Rte. 28					*	*	*
Oyster Pond, Off Rte. 28						*	
Ridgevale Beach, Off Rte. 28					*	*	
HYANNIS							
Kalmus Park, Ocean St.		*			*	*	*
Orrin Keyes Beach, Sea St.		*			*	*	*
Veteran's Park, Ocean St.		*			*	*	*
BARNSTABLE							
Covell Beach, Craigville Beach Rd.		*	*				
Craigville Beach, Off Rte. 28		*			*		
Hamblin's Pond, Rte. 149				*			
Millway Beach, Off Rte. 6A		*				*	
Sandy Neck Beach, Off Rte. 6A		*	*		*	*	*
YARMOUTH							
Bass River Beach, South Shore Dr.		*			*	*	*
Parkers River Beach, South Shore Dr.					*	*	*
Seaview Beach, South Shore Dr.					*	*	

Forests, Preserves & Parks

Barnstable

A 4.8-mile round-trip marked trail at **Sandy Neck** takes you past salt marshes and dunes, leading to the beach. The views of Cape Cod Bay are awesome.

Crocker Neck Conservation Area offers 97 acres of salt marsh to the east and a freshwater marsh to the south. Located on Popponesset Bay.

Yarmouth

The **Botanical Trails of the Historical Society of Old Yarmouth** offer 50 acres of woodland wonder, with oak and pine trees. A small pond sparkles in the sun and a plethora of Cape flora can be seen here, including berry plants, rhododendrons, lace slippers, holly and more. The Botanical Trails are located behind the post office.

In Yarmouth Port, the **Bass Hole Boardwalk** will take you through marshlands and eventually lead you to Gray's Beach. Enjoy the pleasant view of Cape Cod Bay and Chapin Beach in Dennis at the boardwalk's end.

Another boardwalk worth mentioning is the **Yarmouth Boardwalk**, which extends through swamp and marshlands and past beautiful Swan Pond.

Dennis

The **Indian Lands and Conservation Nature Trails** in Dennis offer several trails. You'll find a plethora of Mid-Cape flora, marshlands, and views of Bass River.

A 2½-mile round-trip trail to Cape Cod Bay at Crow's Pasture will take you past wild apple and cherry trees, honeysuckle, and beach plum. Located in East Dennis. Don't miss Scargo

Tower with views of Cape Cod Bay and beyond. A very romantic place. Follow Scargo Hill Road to the tower.

Scargo Lake, in Dennis, offers freshwater swimming and is surrounded by woods. From Route 6A, take Scargo Hill Road to reach the lake.

Bicycling

The **Cape Cod Rail Trail** originates in Dennis. This bike path was originally the track for the old Penn Central Railroad. A 20-mile path will lead you from Dennis to Eastham through Nickerson State Park and past salt marshes, sparkling ponds, cranberry bogs and other typical Cape Cod landscape. The trail begins in South Dennis off Route 6, near Theophilus Smith Road.

Recreation

Tennis

Manning's Tennis Courts, 292 Main Street, Route 28, West Harwich. ☎ 508-432-3958.

Mid-Cape Racquet and Health Club, 193 White's Path, South Yarmouth. ☎ 508-394-3511.

Sesuit Tennis Center, 1389 Route 6A, East Dennis. ☎ 508-385-2200.

Wychmere Harbor Beach and Tennis Club, 710 Main Street, Harwich Port. ☎ 508-430-7012.

Golf

Bass River Golf Course, 62 Highbank Road, South Yarmouth. ☎ 508-398-9079.

Bay Point Country Club, Onset Avenue, Onset. ☎ 800-248-8463.

Bayberry Hills Golf Course, West Yarmouth Road, South Yarmouth. ☎ 508-394-5597.

Dennis Highlands Golf Course, 825 Old Bass River Road, Dennis. ☎ 508-385-8347.

Harwich Port Golf Club, Forest, Harwich Port. ☎ 508-432-0250.

Hyannis Golf Club at Iyanough Hills, Route 132, Hyannis. ☎ 508-362-2606.

Kings Way Golf Club, 64 Kings Circuit, Yarmouth. ☎ 508-362-8870.

Tara Hyannis Golf Course, West End Circle, Hyannis. ☎ 508-775-7775.

Boating

Captain Mike's Seafaris, 36 Ocean Street, Hyannis. ☎ 508-775-1730.

Catboat Rides, Inc., 165 Ocean Street, Hyannis. ☎ 508-775-0222.

Freya Sailing Cruises, Sesuit Harbor, East Dennis. ☎ 508-385-4399.

Hesperus Sailing Cruises, Ocean Street, Dock 16, Hyannis. ☎ 508-790-0077.

Hyannis Whale Watching Cruises, Barnstable Harbor, Hyannis, ☎ 508-362-6088.

Pirate Adventures, 4 Ocean Street, Hyannis. ☎ 508-790-1117.

Starfish Bass River Cruises, 38 Route 28, West Dennis. ☎ 508-760-5100.

Hyannisport Harbor Cruises, Ocean Street Dock, Hyannis. ☎ 508-778-2600. Evening jazz and blues cruises, Sunday afternoon, Sunday Ice Cream "Float" and Saturday Cocktail Cruises.

Entertainment

Music

All sorts of famous people have performed at **The Cape Cod Melody Tent** in Hyannis, including Liza Minelli, Tony Bennett, and Aretha Franklin (to name a few). Located at West Main Street and the West End Rotary. Call ☎ 508-775-9100 for schedule information or consult the local newspaper.

Theater

What was once an Unitarian meeting house (in the early 1800s) is now the home to the **Cape Playhouse** in Dennis. Bette Davis, Julie Harris, Gregory Peck, and Jane and Henry Fonda have all taken part in performances here. Located on Route 6A. Call ☎ 508-385-3838 for further information.

Movies

Airport Cinema, Route 132, Hyannis, ☎ 508-771-4330.

Cape Cod Mall Cinema Center, Cape Cod Mall, Hyannis, ☎ 508-771-1666.

Cape Cinema, Route 6A, Dennis, ☎ 508-385-2503.

Hoyts Cinema, Patriot Square Mall, South Dennis, ☎ 508-394-1100.

Nightlife

Hyannis

The Paddock (piano), West End Rotary, ☎ 508-775-7677.

The Mid-Cape

The Roadhouse Café (jazz), South Street, ☎ 508-775-2386.

Liberty Hall (folk), 2150 Main Street, ☎ 508-428-5662.

Barnstable Village

The Dolphin (jazz and dance music), Route 6A, ☎ 508-362-6610.

Cummaquid

Harbor Point (dancing), off Route 6A, ☎ 508-362-2231.

Yarmouth

Oliver's (country rock), Route 6A, ☎ 508-362-6062.

West Dennis

Christine's (varied venues), Route 28, ☎ 508-394-7333.

Sundancer's (alternative rock and raggae), 116 Main Street, ☎ 508-394-1600.

Dennisport

Clancy's (jazz piano), 8 Upper County Road, ☎ 508-394-6661.

The Improper Bostonian (varied venues), Route 28, ☎ 508-394-7416.

Rum Runner's Café (classic rock and blues), 243 Lower County Road, ☎ 508-398-5673.

Reaching The Mid-Cape

By Car

From New York: Take I-95 through Connecticut to Rhode Island. From Providence, take I-195 East. At Bourne, take Route 25 East over the Bourne Bridge. Follow to Route 6 or Route 6A. Route 6 is faster; Route 6A, prettier.

From Boston: Take Route 3 to the Sagamore Bridge, then follow Route 6 or Route 6A to your Mid-Cape destination.

By Air

The **Barnstable Airport** in Hyannis is serviced by several commercial airlines: **Cape Air** flies from Boston to Hyannis, ☎ 800-352-0714; **US Air Express** offers service to Hyannis from Nantucket, New York and Washington D.C. (seasonal) ☎ 800-428-4322.

By Bus

Plymouth and Brockton Bus Lines: Service from Logan Airport and South Station in Boston to Sagamore, Barnstable, and Hyannis. From the Cape, ☎ 508-775-5524; in Boston, ☎ 617-773-9401.

By Ferry

Hy-Line: Ferry passenger service from Hyannis to Nantucket, and from Hyannis to Martha's Vineyard, from mid-May until October. ☎ 508-778-2600.

The Mid-Cape

Steamship Authority: Year-round automobile and passenger service from Hyannis to Nantucket. ☎ 508-477-8600.

For More Information

Cape Cod Chamber of Commerce, ☎ 508-362-3225.

Hyannis Chamber of Commerce, ☎ 508-755-2201.

Centerville Tourist Information, ☎ 508-771-7509.

Dennis Chamber of Commerce, ☎ 508-395-3568; 508-398-3573 (information booth).

Yarmouth Chamber of Commerce, ☎ 508-387-5311.

The Outer Cape

Having got down the bank and as close to the water as we could, where the sand was the hardest, having the Nauset Lights behind us, we began to walk leisurely up the beach, in a northwest direction, toward Provincetown, which was about 25 miles distant, still sailing under our umbrellas with a strong aft wind, admitting in silence, as we walked, the great force of the ocean steam. The white breakers were rushing to the shore; the foam ran up the sand and then ran back as far as we could see – and we imagined how much further along the Atlantic coast, before and behind us – as regularly, to compare great things with small, as the master of a choir beats time with his white wand, and ever and anon a higher wave caused us hastily to deviate from our path, and we looked back on our tracks filled with water and foam.

~ Cape Cod, Henry David Thoreau, 1817-1862

Imagine long stretches of beaches, summer cottages and sea captain mansions, antiques shops, galleries and more. Some call it the Lower Cape, others call it the Outer Cape. I call it quintessential Cape. The Outer Cape is comprised of the towns of Brewster, Harwich, Chatham, Orleans, Eastham, Wellfleet, Truro, and Provincetown.

The towns of the Outer Cape have much to offer. The liveliest spot is Provincetown, with its galleries, restaurants, and funky downtown area and shops. A favorite vacation place for gays and lesbians, there's more than enough fun and crazy celebrations taking place in Provincetown throughout the summer.

Eastham, Truro, and Wellfleet are more sedate and have retained much of their original rural beauty and charm. Orleans and Harwich have experienced some commercial growth, but continue to offer summer vacationers fun in the sun.

DONNA M. BLACKBURN

My favorites towns on the Outer Cape are Chatham and Brewster. Both towns exude charm with lovely inns, boutiques and restaurants.

Connecting the towns of the Outer Cape and protecting much of its original beauty is the Cape Cod National Seashore. Established in 1961 during the Kennedy Administration, it includes over 27,000 acres of land and 30 miles of ocean coastline.

DONNA M. BLACKBURN

Harwich

$\mathcal{I}$t is the five harbors of Harwich which define the town. Facing Nantucket Sound, Harwich has its share of sailboats, fishing boats, charters and yachts coming in and out of its harbors.

Route 28 somewhat mars the Harwich landscape with overly commercialized shopping centers. However, once off the highway, Harwich affords many panoramic views of the Sound, pretty country lanes, its share of sparkling ponds, cranberry bogs and farmlands.

Romantic Hotels & Inns

❦ Dunscroft-By-The-Sea

Romance is in the air at this wonderful 1920 gambrel-roofed Dutch Colonial. The guest rooms are light and airy, and are decorated in soft pastels. Laura Ashley linens with lace and heart mementos decorate the rooms. The Honeymoon Cottage is particurly romantic and private. The King Suite has a Jacuzzi for two; another suite has a working fireplace. My favorite room was room five, which has a brass canopy, lace quilt, and palladium windows.

The gathering room is cozy, featuring a baby grand piano, an extensive library, and a fireplace. An 18th-century French footed secretary opens to a wonderful collection of heart-shaped items: picture frames, shells, rocks and boxes. You'll also find an original copy of *Lady Chatterley's Lover* displayed here. French doors open onto a summer porch overlooking the garden.

It's just a short walk to a private beach, or head the opposite way to several nice shops and boutiques on Main Street in Harwich Port.

A bountiful full breakfast is served daily. Alyce Cunningham is the quintessential romantic, and she and her husband, Wally, will make sure your stay is a perfect one. Open year-round.

Dunscroft-By-The-Sea
24 Pilgrim Road
Harwich Port, MA 02646
☎ 508-432-0810 or 800-432-4345
Fax 508-432-5134
E-mail alyce@capecod.net
$$$

✦ The Augustus Snow House

The Augustus Snow House is a testament to careful restoration. The 1901 Queen Anne Victorian, with its gabled dormers and wrap-around verandah, exudes the charm of bygone years. As you enter, you'll be in awe at the absolute splendor of the place. Rich Victorian wallpaper adorns the hallways. All of the woodwork has been carefully restored.

The sitting room is beautifully decorated with period piece antiques and portraits of two of the Snow forebearers. The wonderfully intricate oak mantle fireplace gives the room a special romantic feel.

Loving couples will adore Belle's Room, which has a luxury king-size bed and a large sitting area in front of sunny bay windows. There's a Jacuzzi in the bathroom. Another romantic hot spot is Melissa's Room, with its high four-poster queen-size canopy bed and sitting area in front of beautifully carved bay windows. The room's fireplace warms you up on colder evenings.

A full breakfast is served daily in the lovely oak-paneled breakfast room. Be sure to visit the Tea Room, offering a full tea menu and the coziest of atmospheres. Open year-round.

DONNA M. BLACKBURN

The Augustus Snow House
528 Main Street
Harwich Port, MA 02646
☎ *508-430-0528*
Fax 508-432-7995
$$$

The Country Inn

The Country Inn exudes rural charm. The six guest rooms are tastefully decorated with plenty of country-style furnishings and linens. Room four is particularly attractive, featuring slanted ceilings and a king-size bed. Room five has exposed beam ceilings and a working fireplace.

The swimming pool is the perfect place to spend a summer afternoon, or ask for a guest pass to a private beach on Nantucket Sound. The inn's 6½-acre grounds are comprised of woodlands, apples trees, and gardens.

A continental breakfast is served daily. The restaurant and tavern is also quite charming, serving dinner throughout the year. Open year-round.

The Country Inn
86 Sisson Road
Harwich Port, MA 02646
☎ 508-432-2769 or 800-231-1722
$$$

✈ Wequassett Inn

There's nothing quite like the Wequassett Inn, which is comprised of 18 buildings with 104 rooms and suites overlooking Pleasant Bay and Round Cove. Each of the rooms has Early American or country pine furnishings.

The inn offers a full array of recreational opportunities, including a 68-foot heated pool, five all-weather tennis courts, and a dock. You can take lessons at the sailing school or, for those past the novice stage, rent a Hobie Cat or Sunfish and take to the water.

DONNA M. BLACKBURN

The restaurant, the Eben Ryder House, has a long-standing reputation for its excellent cuisine. Open from May until October.

Wequasset Inn
Route 28
Pleasant Bay
East Harwich, MA 02645
☎ *508-432-5400 or 800-225-7125*
$$$$

✈ The Wedgewood House

This handsome, beautifully kept home is the perfect place for lovers to relax and enjoy one another. The building is wonderfully decorated with many family heirlooms and antiques.

DONNA M. BLACKBURN

Billed as a place where you can be "houseguests at your best friend's country home," the Wedgewood House offers just that. Lovers will enjoy the Nantucket Room, which has a slanted ceiling, four-poster bed, whirlpool bath, and private balcony. The sleigh bed and old-fashioned flower wallpaper in the Hyannis Room also spell romance.

The central feature of the Living Room is the nine-foot fireplace, and you will also find an extensive library here. Attached to the living room is a sun porch, where you can relax and sip a cup of tea or coffee as you look out at the gardens.

A full breakfast is served in the formal dining room, which has a crystal chanedlier.

The Wedgewood House is situated on two acres of land adjoining an old cranberry bog and five acres of conservation land. Open year-round.

The Wedgewood House
115 Sisson Road
Harwich Port, MA 02646
☎ *508-432-1378*
$$$

The Gingerbread House

This Victorian establishment was built in 1883, and innkeepers Les and Stacia Kostecki have maintained all of its original whimsy. The three-story house has turrets, gingerbread detailing and more. The rooms' high ceilings and long windows lend a romantic touch.

Breakfast is served in a pretty breakfast room that features an extensive collection of dolls from Poland and other parts of the world.

The gardens are carefully tended by Stacia, with bursts of color all around during the spring and summer. A tea room adjoins the inn, offering tea, sandwiches, and scones every afternoon. Open from April until just before Christmas.

The Gingerbread House
141 Division Street
West Harwich, MA 02671
☎ *508-432-1901 or 800-788-1901*
$$$

The Beach House Inn

This beachfront inn affords spectacular views of Nantucket Sound. The rooms are nicely decorated with period reproductions. The Tower Room and Monomoy Room offer panoramic views of the Sound. The cozy Wychmere Room sports a four-poster canopy and a working fireplace.

The outdoor deck and private beach offer a nice place to relax and enjoy the sun.

A continental breakfast buffet is served daily. Open throughout the year.

The Beach House Inn
4 Braddock Lane
Harwich Port, MA 02646
☎ 508-432-4444 or 800-870-4405
$$$-$$$$

Restaurants

L'Alouette

French restaurants always spell romance, and L'Alouette is no exception. This cozy restaurant has been part of the Harwich Port landscape for over 10 years. Entrées include such delicacies as bouillabaise with lobster, shrimp, scallops, littlenecks, mussels, and fish in a saffron lobster broth or braised lamb shank served with mashed potatoes. Reservations are recommended.

L'Alouette
787 Route 28
Harwich Port
☎ 508-430-0405
$$$$

The Country Inn

The dining rooms here have a definite romantic feel to them, with lots of country charm. Menu selections include an assortment of fish, poultry, and meat dishes. Or consider the "Loving Couple-Dinner For Two," including a special platter with two petite filet mignons, accompanied by four jumbo shrimp scampi, scallops, and lobster claws served on a bed of rice with a Merlot and cracked pepper demi-glace and drawn butter. Follow with a tasty dessert.

The Country Inn
86 Sisson Road
Harwich Port
☎ 508-432-2769
$$$

The Cape Sea Grille

This restuarant is housed in an old sea captain's home and offers a relaxed and elegant dining experience, with creative American cuisine. Choose from such entrées as swordfish piccata with lemon, capers and plum tomato or crunchy tempura shrimp with pineapple/ginger salsa over Asian-style vegetables.

The Cape Sea Grille
31 Sea Street
Harwich Port
☎ 508-432-8534
$$$

Wequasett Inn

This waterfront restaurant is located on Pleasant Bay. The views are panoramic and the restaurant has long been regarded for its excellent food. They specialize in continental and regional cuisine. Choose from sautéed Southwest dusted shrimp on a black bean and shrimp cake or grilled Nantucket scallops, cracked black pepper, parsnip purée in a creamy Chatham lobster sauce.

Wequasett Inn
Route 28
Harwich Port
☎ *508-432-5400*
$$$-$$$$

The Stewed Tomato

The atmosphere here is basic diner, but the food is good and the staff friendly. Serving breakfast and lunch, the restaurant is expanding its menu to include dinner.

The Stewed Tomato
Harwich Center
☎ *508-432-1203*

The Tea Rooms of Harwich

This romantic guide would not be complete without mentioning two wonderful tea houses in Harwich, both well worth a visit. The **Augustus Snow House** and the **Gingerbread House** both serve traditional English teas throughout the summer months.

The Gingerbread House
141 Division Street
West Harwich
☎ *508-349-2596*
$$

The Augustus Snow House
528 Main Street
Harwich Port
☎ *508-430-0528*
$$

Touring Harwich

Harwich offers five harbors. Facing Nantucket Sound, the harbors are busiest in summer, with a full assortment of boats coming in and out from the sea. Harwich is also known for its cranberry business. Every September the town pays homage to the pretty berry during a two-week Cranberry Festival.

Harwich is comprised of seven villages: Harwich, East Harwich, Harwich Port, North Harwich, Pleasant Lake, South Harwich, and West Harwich. Route 28 does somewhat spoil touring Harwich. However, once away from the highway, the town is quite pretty. Harwich Port's Main Street has retained some of its original charm with an assortment of pleasant shops and boutiques. Harwich Center also has an old-fashioned quality to it.

Like the rest of the Cape, Harwich has an extensive maritime history; more than a handful of sea captains built their homes here. Learn more about Harwich's past at the **Brooks Academy Museum**, on Main Street in Harwich Center. This 1844 building was the site of a school that offered some of the region's first courses in navigation. Maritime and Native American artifacts are featured, as are displays of antique glass, photographs, toys, clothing and more. Open from spring to fall. Call ☎ 508-432-8089 for further details.

The prettiest harbor in Harwich, **Wychmere**, was formerly a salt marsh. Prior to the harbor's construction, boats were moored a mile offshore or docked at piers along the coast. Allen Harbor and Saquatucket Harbor were also man-made. Round Cove is the only natural harbor in the town. Consider taking a day-trip to Nantucket Island via Freedom Cruise Lines, located at Saquatucket Harbor.

DONNA M. BLACKBURN

Brewster

I'm a great fan of Brewster. While researching this book, I found myself drawn again and again to this town. Route 6A is pretty wonderful from start to finish, but Brewster, to me, has it all: old stately homes, fine restaurants, forests, ponds and beach, all in close proximity to each other. There's a real sense of community here, too.

Romantic Hotels & Inns

❧ The Brewster Farmhouse Inn

This carefully restored 1850s farmhouse is full of charm and savvy. The building's exterior, with green and white awnings, beckons you to take a peak inside. The two-story Fireplace Gathering Room has lots of light and a great pine table perfect for a chat at tea time or breakfast. The back yard features an expansive sundeck, a heated pool, and a spa overlooking an orchard.

The most romantic offering is the Garden Room, which comes complete with a king-size carved canopy bed, private deck, and bath. A smaller, but still wonderfully cozy room is the third-story Acorn Room. It has dormer ceilings and painted flower stencils. A gourmet breakfast is served in the Gathering Room or, weather permitting, outside on the deck overlooking the pool. Carol and Gary Concors, your friendly hosts, will make sure your visit is first class. Open throughout the year.

The Brewster Farmhouse Inn
716 Main Street
Route 6A
Brewster, MA 02631
☎ 508-896-3910 or 800-892-3910
Fax 508-896-4232
$$$

❧ Captain Freeman's Inn

Light filters through floor-to-ceiling windows, hanging flower pots and rocking chairs rest on the large front porch. The spacious guests rooms are all furnished with four-poster lace crocheted canopy beds.

DONNA M. BLACKBURN

For the romantic, the Luxury Suite offers a private whirlpool spa in an enclosed balcony, a fireplace with a sitting area, and amenities like cable television with VCR, refrigerator, and phone. A large living room entices you to sit and read the paper or visit with new-found friends. Outdoors, you'll find a large pool and some colorful flower and herb gardens that lead down to a lawn set up for crochet and badminton.

Enjoy a gourmet breakfast in the lovely indoor dining room or on the screened-in porch. A scrumptious breakfast is created by the chef and innkeeper, Carol Edmondson. The inn offers cooking school weekends during the off-season. Learn more about healthy gourmet cooking and win your lover's heart.

The Captain Freeman's Inn
15 Breakwater Road
Brewster, MA 02631
☎ 508-896-7481 or 800-843-4664
www.captfreemaninn.com
$$$

Old Manse Inn

The Old Manse Inn is the real thing. It feels old and comfortable. Here, you can imagine what it might have been like to live in another century. Recent renovations have been undertaken by the inn's young and earnest new innkeepers, David and Suzanne Plum. Each room is tastefully decorated with period antiques and offers air-conditioned comfort throughout the summer.

The restaurant has also been redecorated and offers a complimentary full breakfast for guests.

The Old Manse Inn
1861 Main Street
Brewster, MA 02631
☎ 508-896-3149

The Candleberry Inn

The stately Georgian Candleberry Inn stands tall and proud, painted white with green shutters. Manicured lawns surround the property. Are we sure we're not in England?

The innkeepers have done much to maintain the original charm of the inn while adding their own sophisticated touches. The six rooms are pleasantly decorated, each with private bath. Consider the large two-room Dugan Suite or the Snow Room, which has a queen-size four-poster bed, painted wide pine floors, and working fireplace.

A full gourmet breakfast is served daily in the dining room or on the brick porch overlooking the garden. Open year-round.

The Candleberry Inn
1882 Main Street
Brewster, MA 02631
☎ 508-896-3300 or 800-573-4769
www.sunsol.com/candleberry

Old Sea Pines Inn

This building once housed an exclusive boarding school for young ladies. As I entered the large downstairs living room I visualized a beau of yesteryear waiting for his beloved to come downstairs.

Much effort has been made to maintain the inn's history. The upstairs rooms are decorated in period piece antiques and reproductions. The Bickford Room is particularly romantic, with a fireplace and private sun porch. Behind the main house is the North Cottage or "Little Sea Pines." The rooms have been restored and modernized. The Garden Suite is a six-room suite with a kitchenette and fireplace – the perfect retreat for honeymooners.

A full breakfast is served in the formal dining room or, weather permitting, on an outdoor dining deck made cheerful with gingham tablecloths and overloloking the lawns and gardens. Open throughout the year.

The Old Sea Pines Inn
P.O. Box 1070, 2553 Main Street
Brewster, MA 02631
☎ 508-896-6114; Fax 508-896-7387
$$$

Isaiah Clark House

Captain Isaiah Clark built this home over a century ago. Presently, it is an enchanting inn full of simple elegance and charm. The seven guest rooms are attractively furnished with period antiques. Romantics will enjoy the Hattie Mae Room, which features blue-and-white plaid linens and curtains, a suspended canopy bed, and a working fireplace. The Lydia Clark Room is light and airy, with windows overlooking the gardens on three sides.

Enjoy a full American breakfast in the Keeping Room, which has a charming old-fashioned hearth, or outside on the deck. The gardens are particularly romantic. Enjoy five acres of lawn, shade trees, and bountiful flowers. The Innkeepers promise to spoil you. Open year-round.

Isaiah Clark House
1187 Old King's Highway (Route 6A), Box 169
Brewster, MA 02631
☎ *508-896-2223 or 800-822-4001*
Fax 508-896-7054
$$$

Chillingsworth

You'll be in the expert hands of Pat and Nitzi Rabin at this small, intimate inn. Chillingsworth is known primarily for its first-class restaurant, but the three guest rooms upstairs are also worth a visit. The house was built in 1689. Each room is decorated with antiques and reproductions.

Breakfast is served in the dining room, on the outdoor patio, in the gazebo, or in your room. The inn offers guest passes to the nearby Ocean Edge Conference Center. This entitles you to full use of the health club, indoor and outdoor pools, tennis, and 18-hole golf course.

Chillingsworth
2449 Main Street
Brewster, MA 02631
☎ *508-896-3640*
$$$

✦ High Brewster

I fell in love with this place from the moment I arrived. The setting is remarkable, an old inn built high on a bluff overlooking the Lower Mill Pond. Several cottages are on the property, offering guests complete privacy. The inn was built in 1738 and was originally the Nathaniel Winslow Homestead. The well-known and popular **High Brewster Restaurant** occupies the first floor. Upstairs are three guest rooms.

However, the most romantic quarters are the four cottages. The Pond Cottage has a bedroom, efficiency kitchen and a screened-in porch and open deck overlooking the Lower Mill Pond. My favorite is the Barn Cottage. It has a large living

DONNA M. BLACKBURN

room with a fireplace and original ceiling beams, a separate bedroom, loft and private yard. It couldn't be more romantic.

High Brewster
964 Satucket Road
Brewster, MA 02631
☎ *508-896-3536 or 800-203-2634*
Fax 508-896-3734
$$$

Restaurants

Chillingsworth

Chillingsworth has received many awards, including the Forbes Top Forty American Restaurant and the Distinguished

Restaurant of North America. It is the Cape's only Mobil Four Star dining establishment. The bistro is chic and modern with light pouring in from the windows and skylight. I had the grilled swordfish with garlic mashed potatoes and lemon caper butter sauce and savored every bite of it. Other specialties include the grilled lamb chop with risotto and duck breast salad with sun-dried cranberry/raspberry vinaigrette.

In the main dining rooms the atmosphere is more Colonial and formal. If you really want to win your lover's heart, ask for the private dining room. A patio dining room, decorated in soft, muted colors, overlooks the garden. Fresh-cut flowers and candles add to the charm.

Entrée choices include seared salmon with tomato, leeks, orzo, greens and warm mushroom vinaigrette, or seared native sea scallops with spinach, beans, citrus-butter sauce and basil, and other meat and seafood specialties. Reservations required.

Chillingsworth
2449 Main Street
Brewster, MA 02631
☎ *508-896-3640*
$$$

The Brewster Fish House

A local favorite, the Brewster Fish House is small and intimate with fresh local seafood fare. Choose from grilled red snapper achiote, a fresh fillet in a spinach marinade with grilled onion and pineapple, or seasonal crusted flounder sautéed with black and white sesame seeds, served on Asian-dressed bok choy with jasmine rice, and other fish specialties.

The Brewster Fish House
2208 Main Street
☎ *508-896-7867*
$$$

High Brewster

The High Brewster is a wonderful choice for romantics looking for a restaurant which will please both the visual and gastronomical senses. The restaurant's dining rooms are intimate with simple Colonial elegance. The four-course prix-fixe menu is pricey, but the selections are imaginative, including entrées like steamed lobster with fennel and pernod cream served over summer vegetable pilaf and braised endive or rack of lamb dijonnaise with herbed mustard demi-glace and dauphinoise potatoes. Reservations are required.

High Brewster
964 Satucket Road
☎ 508-896-3636
$$$

The Bramble Inn and Restaurant

Another restaurant which has received much praise is the Bramble Restaurant, offering a prix-fixe four-course dinner. Selections include tasty entrées like escalope of venison or seafood curry with lobster, cod, scallops, and shrimp in a light curry sauce accompanied by grilled banana, toasted almonds, coconut, and chutney. Reservations are required.

The Bramble Inn and Restaurant
2019 Main Street
☎ 508-896-7644
$$$

Old Manse Inn and Restaurant

If you're looking for an elegant restaurant with a quiet atmosphere, the recently renovated Old Manse Restaurant is a good choice. Dine by candlelight and enjoy a prix-fixe menu featuring such specialties as shellacked fillet of Atlantic salmon-Szechwan served with eggplant relish fermented in black bean sauce and a purée of chick peas, roasted garlic and cilantro. Or try the stewed monkfish gumbo with shrimp, mussels, and andouille sausage. Restaurateurs and innkeepers David and Suzanne Plum are recent graduates of the Culinary Institute of America, and they've poured their hearts and souls into making your dining experience a memorable one.

The Old Manse Inn
1861 Main Street
☎ *508-896-3149*
$$$

Touring Brewster

Brewster was named after Pilgrim elder William Brewster, one of the *Mayflower* travelers and the first settlers in the area. The town became a mecca for wealthy sea captains, and many of the bed and breakfasts and inns here were formerly the homes of these adventurous men.

At the very heart of Brewster is the **Brewster General Store**. A group of locals gathers here every morning on the outside porch for coffee and a chance to catch up with one another. They are a friendly crew and will happily give you directions and information. You're sure to enjoy shooting the breeze with them. The blue gingham curtains give the store a friendly quality, as does the shiny interior, which has items you can find only in a general store. The building, erected in 1852, was originally a church. Six years later it was transformed into a general store. Since then it has been selling toys, cards, cooking supplies, jams, candies, and lots of small knick-knacks. Located at 1935 Main Street, a trip to the store should definitely be on your itinerary.

The **Unitarian Universalist Church**, at Route 6A and Breakwater Road, was originally called the "Church of the Sea Captains." It was here that sea captains and their families worshipped, although it was then called the First Parish Church. Behind the church is an old burial ground where many of the sea captains are buried.

The **Cape Cod Museum of Natural History** is also located in Brewster. The town is very proud of its museum. For people interested in learning more about the natural history of the Cape, it's a great place to visit. The museum also has several attractive trails leading through a varied terrain of salt

marshes, forest, and beach. Located on Route 6A. Call
☎ 508-896-3867.

History buffs should also consider a visit to the **New England Fire and History Museum** to learn more about the days of yore when firemen chased fires in horse-drawn vehicles. The museum has 35 antique fire engines on display along with other fire-fighting memorabilia. Located at 1439 Main Street, ☎ 508-896-5711.

Be sure to allow time to wander around Brewster's **antique shops** on Route 6A, Old King's Highway.

Legend

According to local legend, the famous sea captain David Nickerson was handed a child while visiting Paris during the French Revolution and asked to raise him in America. He brought the boy to Brewster and raised him as his foster son. The boy was the Last Dauphin of France, the son of Louis XVI and Marie Antoinette. Named René Rousseau by his foster parents, he met an untimely death at the age of 26, lost at sea.

DONNA M. BLACKBURN

Chatham

$\mathcal{I}$t takes a while to reach Chatham, but once you're there you may never want to leave. Chatham is a seaside resort with a lovely main street and beautiful residential areas. Surrounded by Nantucket Sound to the south and the Atlantic Ocean to the east, Chatham affords wonderful water views. This is Cape Cod at its best. If you're looking for a place just minutes away from the beach with shopping and dining galore and want to feel as if you are worlds away from your own hectic life, Chatham is a perfect vacation spot.

Welcome

Romantic Hotels & Inns

✈ Chatham Bars Inn

This seaside resort has been part of the Chatham landscape since 1914. Built on a bluff overlooking the Chatham Harbor, it's a premier place to stay. The inn's restful veranda is where you'll find guests sipping a beverage, reading the newspaper or gazing toward the Atlantic Ocean. The main building has 40 elegant guests rooms and suites, many with fireplaces and balconies offering spectacular views. For complete privacy, stay at one of the private cottages.

A full range of recreational activities are available, including golf, a heated outdoor pool, tennis courts, sailing, and fishing.

The resort's restaurants are long-time favorite dining spots of locals and travelers alike. Open year-round.

The Chatham Bars Inn
Shore Road, Chatham, MA 02633
☎ 508-945-0096 or 800-527-4884; Fax 508-945-5491
E-mail resrvcbi@chathambarsinn.com
$$$$

DONNA M. BLACKBURN

⚘ The Captain's House Inn

The Captain's House Inn offers the best in luxury lodging. The Greek Revival home was built in 1839 by Captain Hiram Harding.

The beautifully appointed guest rooms are stunning. Romantics will enjoy the Lydia Harding Suite, which has a king-size bed, double whirlpool tub, fireplaces in both the sitting room and bedroom, and French doors leading out to a large balcony. The Tradewinds Room has a romantic bow-shaped canopy bed, an almond enamel fireplace, and a private brick patio with rose-covered trellises. The Captain Hiram Harding Room's walnut-paneled walls, beamed ceilings and wood-burning fireplace are distinguished, as is the king-size bed with fine white linens.

Breakfast is served in the dining room on linen-covered tables set with sterling silver and fine china. View the classic English

DONNA M. BLACKBURN

gardens from the room's floor-to-ceiling windows. An afternoon tea is also served daily, complete with freshly baked scones, jams, tarts, and cakes. Open year-round.

The Captain's House Inn
369-377 Old Harbor Road
Chatham, MA 02633
☎ 508-945-0127
Fax 508-945-0866 or 800-315-0728
E-mail capthouse@capecod.net
www.captainhouseinn.net
$$$-$$$$

✈ The Queen Anne Inn

My favorite mix for a inn is one that combines whimsy flair and beauty. The Queen Anne Inn has both. It has been providing an intimate resort vacation to guests since 1874. The sitting rooms and guest rooms are nicely appointed with antiques. Ro-

mantics should consider the Cathedral Ceiling Room, which features a balcony, fireplace, and large hot tub. Or choose the Garden Studio, which also has a balcony and fireplace, plus a Jacuzzi.

The inn has three private clay tennis courts, an outdoor heated pool, a lovely garden, and a spacious indoor spa. Its restaurant, the Earl of Chatham, is popular.

The Queen Anne Inn
70 Queen Anne Road
Chatham, MA 02633
Reservations: ☎ *508-945-0394; outside Massachusetts*
☎ *800-545-INNS*
Fax 508-945-4884
E-mail queenanne@capecod.net
$$$

The Chatham Wayside Inn

Located in the heart of Chatham's historical district, the Wayside Inn offers spacious rooms with lots of old-fashioned charm.

Guest rooms and suites are decorated with country and turn-of-the-century furnishings. Some of the 56 rooms have fireplaces and whirlpool baths. The restaurant is a local favorite.

The Chatham Wayside Inn
512 Main Street
P.O. Box 685
Chatham, MA 02633-0685
Reservations: ☎ 800-391-5734 or 508-945-5550
Fax 508-945-3407
E-mail waysideinn@waysideinn.com
$$$-$$$$

Moses Nickerson House Country Inn

This building was once the home of a sea captain and has retained much of the feel of those by-gone years. Its wide pine floorboards, fireplaces, and antique furnishings lend a warmth to the place, as does the beautiful outdoor garden. Each of the seven rooms have been carefully decorated. Room one has an antique four-poster bed with hand-painted flowers, a fireplace, and French doors opening to the front porch. Room five is also quite romantic, decorated in rose color with blue and green accents. A large bay window overlooks the garden and water fountain.

A full breakfast is served in a glassed-in sunroom with views of the garden. Open year-round.

Moses Nickerson House Country Inn
364 Old Harbor Road
Chatham, MA 02633
☎ 800-628-6972 or 508-945-5859
Fax 508-945-7087
E-mail tmnhi@capecod.net
www.virtualcapecod.com / market / mnickerson /
$$$

The Cranberry Inn

The Cranberry Inn has 18 guest rooms, all furnished with antique and reproduction pieces. The most romantic rooms have beamed ceilings, fireplaces, hand-stenciled wall decorations, four-poster beds, and private balconies. The living room, with its fireplace and baby grand piano, is a good place to meet people. A buffet breakfast and afternoon tea are served daily. Open year-round.

The Cranberry Inn
359 Main Street
Chatham Village, MA 02633
☎ 800-332-4667 or 508-945-9232
Fax 508-945-3769
$$$

The Bradford Inn

The cheerful white exterior and yellow awnings beckon you to come and stay awhile at the Bradford. The Johnathan Grey House features four luxury rooms with Federal period furnishings. A two-bedroom home, the Captain's Hideaway, is perfect for romantics seeking a private tryst. Or consider the Captain's Quarters: Up a steep stairway, you'll find a lovely suite with a four-poster king-size bed, sitting room, fireplace, Jacuzzi, and private deck. The outdoor patio and gardens are reminiscent of the English countryside. An outdoor heated pool provides a great place to relax on a sunny summer afternoon. A full breakfast is served daily. Open year-round.

The Bradford Inn
26 Cross Street
P.O. Box 750
Chatham, MA 02633
☎ 508-945-1030; reservations, 800-CHATHAM
Fax 508-945-9652
www.virtualcapecod.com / market / villageinns /
E-mail azubah@capecod.net
$$$

Restaurants

The Impudent Oyster

This restaurant has been getting a lot of attention for its nouvelle cuisine, and is considered one of the hippest restaurants in the area. While seafood still reigns here, the menu offers some fine imaginative dishes. Consider the scallops San Cristobal, Cape sea scallops broiled en casserole with avocado, tomato, cilantro, and lime and finished with a lemon-butter sauce. Or opt for the pesca fra diavolo, littlenecks, lobster, and assorted fish simmered in a spicy sauce of Italian plum tomatoes, shallots, green peppers, white wine, and herbs, served with fettucine.

The Impudent Oyster
15 Chatham Bars Avenue
☎ *508-945-3545*
$$$

The Chatham Bars Inn

For an elegant dining experience, complete with views of the Chatham Harbor, this inn restaurant can't be beat. It offers continental and American cuisine. Reservations are recommended. Also at the Chatham Bars Inn is the Beach House Grill, set on the water's edge, and The Tavern at the Inner Bar.

The Chatham Bars Inn
Shore Road
☎ *508-945-0096*
$$$$

Champlains Restaurant

This restaurant offers an intimate dining atmosphere in an 1860s sea captain's home. Serving breakfast, lunch, and dinner, the restaurant is also a favorite spot for Sunday brunch. Menu selections include a host of fresh seafood specialties.

Champlains at the Bradford Inn
26 Cross Street
☎ *508-945-9151*
$$$$

Chatham Squire

One of the best ways to measure the success of a Cape Cod restaurant is whether the locals eat there. Chatham Squire is definitely successful! It has a relatively casual atmosphere, serving fresh and tasty seafood.

Chatham Squire
487 Main Street
☎ *508-945-0945*
$$$

Christian's

Housed in a Colonial inn, Christian's has two separate dining rooms. The downstairs dining room is quite pretty with its French-country decor. Upstairs features a wonderful deck overlooking Main Street. Food selections include French and New England fare. Lunch and dinner.

Christian's
443 Main Street
☎ *508-945-3362*
$$$

Touring Chatham

Chatham has been a favorite vacation spot for travelers seeking a way of life long forgotten in other parts of the United States. Chatham has a small central downtown area and many beautiful and quiet residential streets. Surrounded by Nantucket Sound and the Atlantic Ocean, Chatham's beaches are some of Cape Cod's finest.

Chatham was originally called Monomoyick by the Wampanoag Indians. It was settled by a group of Pilgrims in the late 1600s and incorporated in 1712. Initially a farming community, Chatham began to look toward the sea for commerce purposes and continues to thrive as a sea-faring town.

Chatham's **Main Street** is perfect for strolling, dining, and shopping. Small boutiques, galleries, restaurants, and gift shops line the street.

Near the center of town is **Kate Gould Park**. On Friday evenings during the summer months, a crowd gathers here to listen to the renowned Chatham Band.

The town is home to several historic sites, including the **Old Atwood House**. Built in 1752, the house is owned by the Chatham Historical Society. It has a gambrel roof, wide floor planks and a beehive oven in the kitchen. Of particular note is the 1974 Durang Wing collection of seashells from around the world. An herb garden and the old turret and lens from the Chatham Light are on the grounds. Located at 347 Stage Harbor Road. Call ☎ 508-945-2493 for more information.

Also of historical interest is the **Railroad Museum** at the Chatham Railroad Company Station on Depot Road. Learn more about the history of trains through the museum's railroad memorabilia, including train models, a diorama of the 1915 Chatham railroad station and old equipment.

There's never a dull moment at **Chatham's Fish Pier**, where you can watch from the observation deck as fishermen bring in all sorts of treasures from the sea, including lobster, haddock, cod, flounder and more. The pier is located at the corner of Shore Road and Barcliff Avenue.

The **Chatham Light** affords great views of the harbor. The light can be seen from 28 nautical miles and flashes two lights every 10 seconds. Located at James Head Bluff, the lighthouse has survived many storms (check out the famous Chatham Harbor breakthrough caused by a Nor'easter in 1987).

DONNA M BLACKBURN

Orleans

Fifteen miles from Chatham lies Orleans. While parts of Orleans have succumbed to commercialism, it has several nice areas that shouldn't be missed. Of particular charm is the east side of town along Rock Harbor Road, where you'll find a long row of Cape shingled houses, complete with picket fences and pretty gardens. The road will lead you to Rock Harbor, which hosts one of the largest charter fishing fleets in the area. Beach Road leading out to Nauset Beach offers remote beauty. Once at the beach you'll be rewarded with stunning views of the Atlantic Ocean.

Romantic Hotels & Inns

⚘ Morgan's Way

The remoteness of this bed and breakfast is perfect for a romantic getaway. The stunning architecture of the contemporary Cape affords sweeping views of the surrounding woods. The cathedral ceilings with natural oak beams couldn't be more glamourous.

The Greenhouse Room, located on the first floor, is decorated in green, rose and antique white and is furnished with early American reproduction furniture. The room connects to a small greenhouse, opening into the pool and deck area.

Climb the spiral staircase to the Blue Room, decorated in periwinkle blue and white and furnished in ash and light pine.

A secluded poolside guest house with a living room, full kitchen, and loft bedroom is available for weekly rentals.

A full gourmet breakfast is served indoors in the dining area or on the deck overlooking the grounds and gardens.

Morgan's Way Bed and Breakfast
Nine Morgan Way
Orleans, MA 02653
☎ *508-255-0831*
E-mail morganway@capecod.net
www.capecodaccess.com / morgansway /
$$$

✈ The Nauset House Inn

Imagine if love were contagious, and all you needed to catch it was to be around other people in love. Visit the Nauset House, owned by the Diane and Al Johnson and their daughter and son-in-law Cindy and John Vessella. The family spent considerable time making this inn perfectly romantic for everyone who visits.

The house was originally a farm house, built in the early 1800s. The 14 guest rooms are decorated in country splendor, complete with hand-painted furniture and country quilts. The 1907 Lord and Burnham glass conservatory was added in 1978 and is by far one of the coziest spots, featuring flowering plants and wicker furniture.

Diane Johnson is an accomplished artist, as evidenced by the decor. She's also a wonderful cook. Join her and her family for a full breakfast and an afternoon repast. Open from April through October.

The Nauset House Inn
Beach Road
P.O. Box 774
East Orleans, MA 02643
☎ *508-255-2195*
www.virtualcapecod.com / market / nausethouse /
$$$

The Parsonage Inn

The Parsonage has a refined elegance to it. The 1770 Cape house is well maintained, and careful attention to detail gives it a special feel. The eight rooms have been decorated with antiques and reproduction furnishings. A picket fence surrounds the property and a small intimate brick patio offers guests a nice place to linger.

A buffet breakfast is served daily, and you can also enjoy afternoon tea in the parlor/library. Open throughout the year.

The Parsonage Inn
202 Main Street
P.O. Box 1501
East Orleans, MA 02643
☎ *508-255-8217*
$$$

The Orleans Waterfront Inn

The Orleans Inn was built in 1875 by Aaron Snow for his wife and seven children. It was transformed from a private residence to a boarding house, then to a hotel. Its most recent transformation includes a $2 million renovation. The current owners, the Maas family, have given special consideration to maintaining the inn's earlier charm. Many of the guest rooms afford lovely views of the water. Romantics will enjoy a waterfront suite, complete with a king-size bed and living room. A continental breakfast is served in the dining room, which overlooks the town cove. Open year-round.

The Orleans Waterfront Inn
3 County Road
P.O. Box 188
Orleans, MA 02653
☎ *508-255-2222*
$$$-$$$$

The Hillhourne House

A room with a view will be yours at the Hillhourne House. Situated on Pleasant Bay, the house was erected in 1798. During the Civil War it was one of several stops on the Underground Railroad, used by escaped slaves from the South on their way up to freedom in Canada.

Each room is decorated with antiques and has a country flair. Romantics will enjoy the privacy of the Carriage House, which has two double bedrooms, a kitchen, and a large living room with a fireplace. A complimentary continental breakfast is served daily. Open year-round.

Hillhourne House
P.O. Box 190
Route 28
South Orleans, MA 02662
☎ *508-255-0780*
$$-$$$

The Ship's Knee Inn

The nautical quality of this inn can't be missed. The ship's knee is a block of wood with a natural angular shape or cut used to fasten and strengthen the corners of wooden vessels; several are on display. The gray-shingled restored captain's house offers 19 guest rooms, all decorated in a nautical style with hand-painted trunks, old clipper ship models, braided rugs, and four-poster beds.

The swimming pool and tennis court offer outdoor fun and the Nauset Beach is almost at its doorstep. A continental breakfast is served daily. Open year-round.

The Ship's Knee Inn
186 Beach Road
P.O. Box 756
East Orleans, MA 02643
☎ *508-255-1312*
Fax 508-240-1351
$$$

Restaurants

The Captain Linnell House

The dining rooms at The Captain Linnell House are small and cozy. Antiques and lace give the restaurant a special romantic feel. The menu offers such entrées as duckling roasted with a raspberry, clove, and honey glaze, or farfalle pasta, lobster, fresh oregano, plum tomato, and a touch of cream. The Sunday brunch is scrumptious.

The Captain Linnell House
137 Skaket Road
☎ *508-255-3400*
$$$

The Old Jailhouse Tavern

Formerly a jailhouse, this restaurant is a local favorite. The menu is divided into categories: Light Sentence, Small Time, Big Time, and The Line-up. It's not a romantic place and the food is your basic tavern fare, but you'll have fun telling the folks at home you've had more than bread and water in a jailhouse.

The Old Jailhouse Tavern
28 West Road
☎ *508-255-JAIL*
$$

DONNA M. BLACKBURN

Barley Neck Inn

Housed in a 1857 sea captain's mansion, the restaurant's four dining rooms serve dinner throughout the summer months. The Taylor Room is cozy, with only five tables. The menu is imaginative. Recent offerings included pan-roasted duck served with duck liver flan, roasted potatoes, baby vegetables, and a red wine, vinegar, and honey sauce, and rainbow trout (farm-raised in West Barnstable) sautéed with almonds, butter, parsley, and lemon, and served with polenta and asparagus.

Barley Neck Inn
5 Beach Road
☎ *508-255-0212*
$$$

Touring Orleans

Orleans is rich in history. The town was named after Louis-Phillippe de Bourbon, the Duke of Orleans and king of France from 1830 until 1848. He visited the area while exiled from France during the French Revolution. According to legend, the townspeople were looking for a new name for the area, and duly named it after him.

Orleans has had its share of military skirmishes. In the War of 1812, the British demanded that the town pay them $1,000 or they would destroy the town's saltworks. The townspeople refused, a battle ensued, and they forced the British from their soil. Orleans wasn't as fortunate during World War I. In fact, Orleans carries the distinction of being the only town in the United States to have suffered a loss during a World War. In 1918, a German submarine surfaced and fired on several barges, sinking them.

Several points of interests in Orleans are worthy of a stop. The **French Cable Station Museum** offers modern communication enthusiasts a chance to see how France and the United States once corresponded. It was at this site that a transcontinental cable originated, connecting France to the United States. Important messages were sent here and then forwarded to a New York City office. Learn more about this old-fashioned form of communication at the museum, open throughout the summer months. Located at 41 South Orleans Street. Call ☎ 508-240-1735 for more information.

Also of historical note is the **Johnathan Young Windmill**, where salt was made from saltwater. Here you can watch demonstrations of the windmill as it pumps saltwater into shallow vaults. Open during the summer season. Follow Route 6A to Town Cove. Call ☎ 508-240-2484 further details.

Rock Harbor affords spectacular views of the Atlantic Ocean and is the place to go to catch a **charter fishing** boat. The neighborhood leading to Rock Harbor is quite pleasant and reminiscent of a quieter time in Orlean's past.

Eastham

$\mathcal{G}$ateway to the Cape Cod National Sea Shore, Eastham is a quiet town with several nice beaches, a host of freshwater ponds, and lots of wide-open space for nature lovers. Route 6 runs through the middle of the town and, to a certain extent, spoils Eastham for people passing through it. However, by turning off onto the side roads, you can reach Cape Cod Bay to the west and the Atlantic Ocean to the east. Eastham also has several interesting historical sites worthy of a visit.

DONNA M. BLACKBURN

Romantic Hotels & Inns

The Overlook Inn

This cheerful yellow Victorian has a tremendous amount of character. Built by Captain Barnabus Chipman as a wedding gift for his wife Sarah, the restored family-run inn still shows its original charm and them some.

Innkeepers Ian and Nan Aitchison and their two sons have created a lively place to stay with plenty of old antiques. The rooms are spacious, with windows overlooking the garden. The Aitchisons, formerly from Scotland, are world travelers, and there are items from Africa, Brazil, and from their native land. Their son's bold modern artwork adorns the walls.

Several nice parlors downstairs offer guests a chance to relax and chat. A billiard room is also available.

A full breakfast is served in the dining room. In the afternoon, enjoy a repast of scones and assorted teas. Open year-round.

The Overlook Inn
P.O. Box 771
3085 Country Road (Route 6)
Eastham, MA 02642-0771
☎ 508-255-1886
Fax 508-240-0345
$$$

The Whalewalk Inn

This 1830 whaling master's home is situated on three acres of land near Rock Harbor. Simple elegance and careful attention to detail is seen throughout the inn. Antique furnishings from England, France, and Denmark decorate the common rooms. The guest house is particularly romantic, offering cathedral ceilings and exposed beams. The four Carriage House rooms

DONNA M. BLACKBURN

have queen-size beds, a sitting area with a fireplace, and individual decks or patios. Several of the rooms have whirlpool baths for two.

A full breakfast is served daily. Open from April through November.

The Whalewalk Inn
220 Bridge Road
Eastham, MA 02642
☎ *508-255-0617*
$$$

 # Touring Eastham

Considered the gateway to the Cape Cod National Seashore, Eastham offers summer fun with lots of pretty country lanes, ponds, and panoramic views of Cape Cod Bay and the Atlantic Ocean.

The town was originally home to the Nauset Indians. In 1651, it was incorporated by a group of Pilgrims who settled here. Like the rest of the region, Eastham has relied heavily on the fishing business. A thriving saltworks industry was established here in the late 1800s. Eastham was also once known as the Asparagus capital of the world.

Several historical sites are worthy of a visit. The **Swift-Daley House** is a fully restored Cape house with a bow roof. It offers a glimpse of bygone years through its Colonial-era furnishings and restored pumpkin-pine woodwork and wide-board floors. Each of the downstairs rooms has a fireplace. Wedding gowns and trousseaus from a century ago on display will catch a romantic's eye, as will the beaded ceremonial quilt. Located on Route 6. Call ☎ 508-255-0788 for more information.

Also of note is the **Old Schoolhouse Museum**, ☎ 508-255-0333. While modern day schools look more like office buildings or factories, this is a one-room schoolhouse. In addition the museum has a display of U.S. Life Saving Service records and a collection of whale jawbones. Located across from the Cape Cod National Seashore Salt Pond Visitor Center, the museum is open weekday afternoons throughout the summer.

The **Eastham Windmill** is the oldest windmill on the Cape. Recently renovated, the it sits in the park on Route 6 at Samoset Road.

Follow the road to the National Seashore past the **Captain Edward Penniman House**, built in 1868. The house's mansard roof and cupola are reminiscent of French Second Empire architecture.

As you travel further down the road, you'll arrive at the entrance to the **Cape Cod National Seashore**. Trails will lead you through the Nauset Marsh and Salt Pond, an area rich in Eastern seaboard flora and fauna. The Salt Pond Visitor Center is the entryway to Cape Cod National Seashore. Here you can get information on trails and hikes throughout the area, guided walks and tours, boat excursions, lectures, and demonstrations. A museum on the premises showcases whaling and saltworks history, local artifacts and more. Located off Route 6. Call ☎ 508-255-3421 for further information.

The red and white **Nauset Light** continues to beam its light out to sea, but her two sisters are stilled. Once called the "Three Sisters," three brick lighthouses were built in 1892 on a bluff in Eastham. Due to shifting underwater sandbars, the cliffs eroded and all of the three sisters dropped into the sea. They were rebuilt, this time as wooden structures. Moved once more in the early part of the century, the sisters were finally reunited by the National Park Service, placing them in their present, safer location. The Salt Pond Visitor Center (☎ 508-255-3421) conducts tours to the lighthouses throughout the summer.

Wellfleet

For some, Wellfleet is synonymous with oysters, for others it's home to a community of writers and artists. Wellfleet has enjoyed the benefits of careful planning and development, and now offers a mix of open land, lovely Cape homes, and a downtown area with fine restaurants, art galleries, and shops.

D. M. BLACKBURN

Romantic Hotels & Inns

The Inn at Duck Creeke

Located in Wellfleet's Historic District and with views of Duck Pond, the Inn at Duck Creeke offers a wonderful blend of history and modern ammenities. The Captain's House, built in the early 1800s, is one of the four buildings comprising the inn. The 25 guest rooms are decorated with country antiques and lace curtains. Many of the bathrooms have claw-foot tubs. Additional rooms are located in the Saltworks Cottage and Carriage House.

The screened porch and veranda are good spots to unwind. A contiental breakfast is served daily.

The inn's two restaurants are very popular. Sweet Seasons overlooks the rush-bordered pond and is considered one of the most romantic restaurants in the area. The Tavern Room's bar is made from a collection of period local marine charts. It is the oldest tavern in town. Open from mid-May to mid-October.

The Inn at Duck Creeke
P.O. Box 364
Wellfleet, MA 02667
☎ 508-349-9333
Web page: www.capecod.net/duckinn
$$$

Winterwood Bed and Breakfast

Imagine telling the folks back home that you stayed at a barn during your stay on Cape Cod. As your friends begin to feel sorry for you, tell them that your stay was in the barn's Garden Suite, complete with a king-size bed, cathedral ceilings, and a whirlpool overlooking gardens. Or tell them that you stayed in the Hayloft, which has vaulted ceilings and skylights.

The Winterwood was originally a barn, built in the 1850s. Converted in 1986, it is now a small but intimate B&B.

Abutting the National Seashore, the property has four acres of secluded pine forest to explore. A fresh continental breakfast is served daily on the outdoor decks or in the privacy of your own room. Not bad barn accomodations. The inn is open from April until November.

> *Winterwood Bed & Breakfast*
> *2160 Long Pond Road*
> *Wellfleet, MA 02667*
> ☎ *508-349-6737*
> *$$$*

Restaurants

Aesop's Tables

Dine in this 18th-century restaurant and feast on Wellfleet oysters and other seafood specialties. The bouillabaisse is the dish everyone talks about. The restaurant's porch offers seating during the summer and overlooks the town's center.

> *Aesop's Tables*
> *316 Main Street*
> ☎ *508-349-6450*
> *$$*

Sweet Seasons

There's nothing better than a dining room with a view. This restaurant, housed in the Inn at Duck Creeke, offers views of Duck Creek. It has a cozy atmosphere and offers seafood, fowl, and meat food selections. Choose from such entrées as Chatham cod, oven-poached cod with fresh Provencal herbs, sliced garlic and caper salsa on mixed greens or tender chicken sautéed with asparagus ravioli in a fresh sage, light cream, and vermouth sauce.

Sweet Seasons
East Main Street
☎ *508-349-6535*
$$$

Painter's

This restaurant is receiving a lot of attention for its imaginative cuisine. Choose from an eclectic selection, such as Thai scallops in red curry-coconut sauce, seasonal vegetables over cappellini, or pan-seared sesame/mustard-encrusted tuna with soy, wasabi and basmati rice.

Painter's
50 Main Street
Wellfleet
☎ *508-349-3003*
$$

 ## Touring Wellfleet

Wellfleet's Main Street looks like an Edward Hopper painting, reminiscent of a time when American towns had a central downtown area. Less commercial than Provincetown or Chatham, Wellfleet's downtown is a mix of shops, restaurants, and art galleries.

Wellfleet's **First Congregational Church** is famous for its steeple clock, which, according to legend, is "the only clock in the world that strikes ship's time." The interior of this 1850 Greek Revival building is stunning, with pale blue walls, a brass chandelier hanging from a gilt ceiling rosette, and curved pews forming an amphitheater. Sunday evening concerts are held here throughout the summer. ☎ 508-349-6877.

Wellfleet's **Historical Society Museum** is also located downtown, exhibiting antique furnishings, clothes, and needlework. Wellfleet's maritime history is chronicled here, including stories and items from famous shipwrecks, paintings and more. Open throughout the summer months. Call ☎ 508-349-9157 for more information.

The town's fishing and boating industries are alive and well. At the **Wellfleet Pier** you will find an assortment of fishing boats, yachts, sailboats, and charter boats busily going about their business.

Marconi Station, located on the Atlantic Ocean, is the site of the first transatlantic wireless station built on United State's soil. Important messages were communicated to and from Europe, beginning in 1903. Although little remains of the original buildings, the Cape Cod National Seashore headquarters is stationed here. A 1¼-mile trail leading to the White Cedar Swamp begins at the parking lot, next to a trail that leads to Marconi Beach.

The **Massachusetts Audubon Wellfleet Bay Sanctuary** is a 1,000-acre refuge for over 250 species of birds. This is a particularly pretty area.

Truro

Truro remains largely unspoiled and offers visitors a relaxing vacation where the most important decision is how to spend the day as lazily as possible.

DONNA M. BLACKBURN

Welcome

Romantic Hotels & Inns

Parker House

The Parker House is laden with history. Built in the early 1800s, the classic, full Cape has been in the same family for four generations. A portrait of the family's forebearer, Captain Elijah Cobb, hangs proudly on the wall, as do other items from the family's history.

Guest rooms are bright and airy. They are decorated with early New England furnishings. A continental breakfast is served daily early or late.

The Parker House
P.O. Box 1111
Truro, MA 02666
☎ *508-349-3358*
$$$

The Moorlands

The Moorlands is a dream come true for Skipper Eval and her husband, Bill. The house was once owned by her great uncle, but was lost to other owners. The Evals reclaimed the property several years ago and have been doting on it ever since.

The grand old Victorian is located on a quiet country road. Upon entering, take note of the faux marble floors, staircase, and dining room table. Bill's colorful modern artwork creates a contrast with many antique and Victorian memorabilia found in the common rooms. The Music/Gathering Room is quiet during the day, but don't be surprised if you find Bill and his friends jamming a jazz tune together at night.

The inn features five guest rooms, two cottages, and the Carriage House Suite. The cozy Carriage House has been restored and now offers a full kitchen, living room, and an upstairs bedroom. You can enjoy your own Jacuzzi in the private courtyard adjacent to the Carriage House.

The guest rooms in the main house are also quite whimisical. The Honeymoon Suite has a delightful feather bed adorned with a white-and-blue embroidered quilt, rounded windows, a sitting room, and a deck. The Penthouse features a cathedral ceiling, a cozy sleeping alcove, a complete kitchen, and deck.

Outside you will find a second Jacuzzi for guests. Occasionally, the Evals will organize a croquet game (bring white clothing to set the mood). Open year-round.

The Moorlands
P.O. Box 38411
Hughes Road
North Truro, MA 02652-0384
☎ 508-487-0663
Fax 508-487-1426
$$$

Restaurants

Whitman House

This restaurant's country atmosphere has been a long-time favorite for romantics. Colonial elegance is the restaurant's signature. Traditional seafood and meat dinners are served during the summer months.

Whitman House
Route 6
Truro
☎ 508-487-1740
$$$$

Touring Truro

Truro's downtown area consists of a post office, town hall, library, and police station. While the town contains 43 square miles, it has the smallest year-round population on the Outer Cape. All of which is to say, it's definitely off the beaten path.

Enjoy the breathtaking view from the Highland Light, also referred to as the Cape Cod Light. The original Highland Light was built in 1798 and was powered by whale oil lamps. The existing lighthouse was built in 1857. It was the last lighthouse in the US to become automated.

Next door to the lighthouse is the **Truro Historical Museum**. Housed in a former turn-of-the-century summer hotel and specializing in 17th-century artifacts, the museum pays homage to the Cape's maritime past, evidenced by its collection of fishing and whaling items, ship models, and a pirate's chest. Located on Lighthouse Road and open throughout the summer months. Call ☎ 508-487-3397 for more information.

Provincetown

At the very tip of the Cape lies Provincetown. By far one of the liveliest spots on the Cape, there's no such thing as a dull moment here. Provincetown is known for its art galleries, nightlife, and restaurants, in to the remote beauty of the beaches and sand dunes just a short distance away.

In the summer the pulse of Provincetown quickens. The town swells with an estimated 90,000 travelers touring the area. However, during the off-season, Provincetown becomes a sleepy fishing village.

Those who call Provincetown their home come from many walks of life. Year-round residents include Portuguese families, fishermen, artists, and writers. Provincetown also supports a strong gay and lesbian community.

DONNA M. BLACKBURN

Romantic Hotels & Inns

Provincetown is full of wonderful places to stay. It's impossible to include all of the town's lodging in this book, but I'd safely say that you can't go wrong no matter where you stay. Here are a couple of my favorites:

✈ Land's End Inn

It's like walking into a museum, a mad artist's home, or something not of this world. More specifically, Land's End Inn is magical. Built at the turn of the century for Boston merchant Charles Higgins, much of his Oriental wood collection, carvings, stained glass, and antiques remain. Like a Victorian doll house, the inn is full of wondrous toys, statues, and whimsical furnishings.

DONNA M. BLACKBURN

The gardens are also quite exquisite. The property faces Cape Cod Bay and has awesome views in every direction. Sixteen rooms are available, all with private baths. The Tower Room and Loft Suite get top billings from romantics.

The inn is now owned by the David Adam Schoolman Trust. David Schoolman was the founder and innkeeper of the inn from 1972 to 1995. Proceeds from the business support the Provincetown Theater and Provincetown Academy of the Performing Arts.

Land's End Inn
22 Commercial Street
Provincetown, MA 02657
☎ *508-487-0706 or 800-276-7088*
$$$

🦅 The Sandpiper Beach House

As you enter the Sandpiper Beach House, you'll know you have arrived at a very romantic spot. The main sitting room is wall-papered with seascape scenes. A breeze quietly plays with the curtains while visitors sip a cup of tea or coffee as they look out at Cape Cod Bay.

The eight guest rooms in the main house are light and airy, and several have views of the bay. My favorite was the Truro room, which has a queen-size four-poster bed, bay windows and a deck. The inn also has five beach units facing the sea, each with a lovely terrace, umbrella and lounge chairs. The Sandpiper offers free guest passes to the neighboring Boatslip Beach Club's

DONNA M. BLACKBURN

pool. Conveniently located in downtown Provincetown, this is a great bet.

The Sandpiper Beach House
165 Commercial Street
P.O. Box 646
Provincetown, MA 02657
☎ *508-487-1928; reservations, 800-354-8628*
www.provincetown.com / sandpiper
E-mail sandpiper@ provincetown.com
$$$

⌇ Windamar House

This stately sea captain's home has been beautifully maintained and lovingly cared for by its owner, Betty Adams. Windamar has six guest rooms, each decorated with flowered wallpapers and matching hand-stitched quilts.

—DONNA M. BLACKBURN

Romantics should consider the Penthouse apartment, which comes complete with a view of Cape Cod Bay. It has cathedral ceilings, exposed beams and an oversize skylight. The room is decorated in antique wicker and pine furnishings. The studio apartment also lends itself to romance with large windows overlooking the English garden.

Located outside of downtown (it's about a 15-minute walk), the Windamar offers a quiet respite from the action in Provincetown.

Windamar House
568 Commercial Street
Provincetown. MA 02657
☎ *508-487-0599*
$$$

The Captain and His Ship

You have entered another time and place at the Captain and His Ship. This elegant inn has all the charm of a turn-of-the-century deluxe hotel. The rooms are spacious, with high ceilings, and are decorated with ornate period antiques. All rooms are air-conditioned and have a color television, VCR, phone and refrigerator. A continental breakfast is served during the summer season. Open year-round. The Captain and His Ship is located near downtown.

The Captain and His Ship
164 Commercial Street
Provincetown, MA. 02657
Reservations ☎ *508-487-1850*
☎ *800-CAPT-2278*
$$$

The Prince Albert Guest House

Named after Queen Victoria's husband, and keeping in the tradition of the Victorian era, this guest house is a testament to good taste. It has eight lovely rooms, many with water views. Romantics will enjoy room #7, which offers rooftop views of

Provincetown and the monument. Or consider the Garden Room, with its own private entrance and patio.

The rooms are equipped with air-conditioning, color television/VCR and refrigerator. Enjoy the handsome brick garden. Open year-round.

> *The Prince Albert Guest House*
> *166 Commercial Street*
> *Provincetown, MA 02657*
> ☎ *508-487-0859 or 800-992-0859*
> *Fax 508-946-1533*
> *$$$*

Somerset House

If you want to be where the action is, consider staying at the Somerset House. This cheerful yellow guest house with green shutters is located in the middle of town. It has a wonderful flower-filled garden and patio facing the street. The interior of the house is nicely decorated in Victorian style. For the discerning romantic, the Somerset Suite is the best choice.

A continental breakfast is served daily. Open year-round.

> *Somerset House*
> *378 Commercial Street*
> *Provincetown, MA 02657*
> ☎ *800-575-1850 or 508-487-0383*
> *somrsethse@aol.com*
> *$$*

Lamplighter Inn

This cozy, friendly inn is located away from downtown, giving its visitors a reprieve from the action of Provincetown. Several suites offer nice views of the bay. The Garden Suite in back is particularly private and comfortable. A large rooftop deck has a 360° view of the surrounding area.

A continental breakfast is served daily, but the inn's crowning culinary glory is the double chocolate Oreo brownies served later in the day.

Lamplighter Inn
26 Bradford Street
Provincetown, MA 02657
☎ *508-487-2529*
$$$

Restaurants

The Martin House

This restaurant continues to be hailed as the most romantic dining experience in town. The twinkling lights from the outdoor garden dining room are inviting, and the intimate indoor dining rooms are just as attractive. The menu changes each season with up to six specials every night. A sample speciality is crab meat martini, Maine crab meat layered with cucumber, watercress and avocado crème fraiche. Or try a smoked duck breast quesadilla with roasted pineapple and tomato salsa.

The Martin House
157 Commercial Street
☎ *508-487-1327*
$$$$

The Dancing Lobster Cafe Trattoria

Ask a local to rate the restaurants, and the Dancing Lobster would more than likely get first place. This restaurant has elevated seafood dining to a new level. The menu is imaginative, influenced by traditional Italian cuisine. The *zuppa di pesce* (Italian seafood stew) is a tasty treat. The restaurant's interior is romantic. Large windows offer great views of the harbor.

The Dancing Lobster Cafe Trattoria
9 Ryder Street
☎ *508-487-0900*
$$$

Café Edwige

Another local favorite, this restaurant is known for its imaginative nouvelle cuisine. The walls are adorned with artwork by local artists and there's an outdoor deck overlooking the bay.

Café Edwige
333 Commercial Street
☎ *508-487-2008*
$$$

The Mews

This elegant restaurant offers gourmet seafood, meat and vegetarian cuisine. Consider the Mews Parisian bouillabaisse, billed as a "generous blend of white fish, shrimp, mussels, scallops, clams, and calamari in a delicately seasoned broth," or the four cheese polenta lasagne, with provolone, mascarpone, and parmesan layered with gorgonzola, portabello mushrooms, spinach and roasted red peppers.

The main dining room has a lovely view of the bay while an upstairs piano bar serves lighter fare. Open for lunch, dinner and Sunday brunch.

The Mews
429 Commercial Street
☎ *508-487-1500*
$$$

Cactus Garden

South-of-the-border delights are offered here throughout the day and into the evening. Indoor seating is available, but the outdoor patio is much more fun for people-watching. This is a great place for brunch.

The smoked salmon empanadas are exquisite, a mixture of Norwegian salmon blended together with cream cheese, plum tomatos, capers and red onions baked in a flaky pastry. It's out of this world!

The Outer Cape

The Cactus Garden
186 Commercial Street
☎ *508-487-6661*
$$

The Lobster Pot

The menu is good old New England seafood and it can't be beat for variety. Order the clam bake and be prepared to feast like a king. Reservations are encouraged.

The Lobster Pot
321 Commercial Street
☎ *508-487-0842*
$$$-$$$$

 ## Touring Provincetown

The defining moment of Provincetown's history occurred in 1620 when the Pilgrims landed here and stayed for about a month before settling in nearby Plymouth.

Upon arriving in Provincetown, the 41 men aboard the *Mayflower* signed the Mayflower Compact, the first document declaring a democratic form of government in America. Provincetown is proud of its Pilgrim heritage and several monuments commemorate this event. The **Pilgrim Monument** can be seen for miles, stretching 225 feet into the sky. Walk up 116 steps and 60 ramps for a wonderful panoramic view of the area. A museum that focuses on the town's history is housed at the base of the monument. Learn more about the town's whaling days and hear the stories of several famous shipwrecks which took place off the shores of Provincetown. Open 9 am to 5 pm, throughout the season. Call ☎ 508-487-1310 for more information.

Other tributes to the Pilgrims' stay are the **Mayflower Compact Plaque**, carved by sculptor Cyrus Dalin, located in the park behind the town hall, and the bronze **Pilgrim Plaque** at the site of the first landing of the Pilgrims, at the west end of Commercial Street.

During the Revoluntionary War, the British controlled Provincetown Harbor, using the port to sail to and from Boston. Provincetown remained relatively quiet until, like the rest of the Cape, the town began to flourish during the whaling days. Provincetown also manufactured salt during the early 1800s, with windmills lining the shore and pumping the salt from the seawater. Provincetown was the most populated town on the Cape in the late 1800s, having over 5,000 residents.

Float Your House

Of historical note is the moving of a house from Long Point to the West End. Long Point, the strip of sand across the harbor that forms the very tip of the Cape, was once the home of a settlement of fishermen and their families. The families had many difficulties transporting fuel and supplies to the area, with poor weather conditions playing a large role. So they decided to move, so they floated their homes across the bay to the West End of town. Today you can recognize these homes by their blue plaques commemorating their trek across the waters.

Lured by the lucrative fishing opportunities, Portuguese from the Azores began to arrive in Provincetown. The town continues to support a strong Portuguese community.

The fishing industry still thrives in Provincetown,as evidenced by the fish brought in at **MacMillian Wharf**. Here you also find whale-watching boats and fishing charters with daily excursions.

It was the arrival of the Old Colony Railroad in 1873 (as well as passenger boats from Boston at about the same time) that first brought tourists to the area.

The **Seth Nickerson House**, at the corner of Commercial and Soper Streets, is the oldest building in town. Also of note is the **octagonal house** built in 1850, at 74 Commercial Street.

Charles Hawthorne was one of the first artists to move to Provincetown. In 1899 he established the Cape Cod School of Art in Provincetown, and artists came from around the world. Provincetown continues to attracting artists, and the East End is lined with galleries. The prestigious **Provincetown Art Association and Museum** is also here. The museum has over 1,600 permanent pieces and several changing exhibits. Located at 460 Commercial Street, it's open daily throughout the summer. Call ☎ 508-487-1750 for more information.

Writers and journalists jumped on the bandwagon and began moving to Provincetown, forming the **Provincetown Players** and several other production companies. The plays were controversial and often explored social and political issues. Eugene O'Neill joined the Players in 1916. Good theater is still part of Provincetown's identity, and excellent shows are put on by the Provincetown Theatre Company and Provincetown Repertory Theatre.

The **Fine Arts Work Center** (FAWC) sponsors 10 writers and 10 artists each summer. The FAWC offers readings, exhibitions and other events throughout the season. Housed in the former Day's Lumber Yard Studios, the center was built to provide struggling artists with a place to stay and work. Located at 24 Pearl Street; call ☎ 508-487-9960 for a schedule of events and for information on their workshops in writing and the visual arts.

Provincetown has several lighthouses, all built more than a century ago. The 1827 **Long Point Lighthouse** beams its light visible for eight nautical miles. **Race Point Lighthouse** has a 41-foot beacon and flashes a white light every 10 seconds. This lighthouse has been a Provincetown fixture since 1816. The newer **Wood End Lighthouse** is 45 feet tall and was built in 1873.

Just north of town you'll find the remote beauty of the **Province Land**, now part of the National Seashore.

Annual Events

February

Year-Rounders Festival in Provincetown is a testament to the town's spirit – even in the cold winter, there's still a reason to party. This event includes wining, dining and generally getting-down together. Held at the Town Hall at 260 Commercial Street. Call ☎ 508-487-3424 for further details.

April

Brewster in Bloom pays homage to the beautiful delicate daffodil. This event is held on the last weekend in April and includes inn tours, a golf tournament, road race, parade and arts and crafts festival. Call ☎ 508-896-8088 for a listing of events.

May

The Cape-wide **Maritime Week** celebrates the Cape's maritime history with a number of activities throughout the area. Most of the lighthouses are open to the public, and there's walks, tours and lectures to attend. Call ☎ 508-362-3838 for further details.

June

Cape Heritage Week is also a Cape-wide event with an emphasis on the Cape's cultural, historical and environmental heritage.

Outdoor walks and tours are part of the fun, as are canoe rides. Open houses and lectures are sponsored by a number of Cape towns. Call ☎ 508-888-1233 for a listing of activities.

The zany, annual drag-a-thon, **Sisters in the Name of Love**, raises money for the Provincetown AIDS Support Group and for Helping Our Women. ☎ 508-487-3424.

Provincetown Portuguese Festival and The Blessing of the Fleet takes place the last weekend in June, with a procession of boats passing through the harbor. Provincetown loves a party, and there are plenty of celebrations on dry land at this time too. This 50-year-old ceremony blesses the town's ships to guarantee safe passage. A Sunday Mass at St. Peter's Church is followed by a parade to Fisherman's Wharf. Call ☎ 508-487-3424 for further details.

Brewster sponsors the **Brewster Historical Society Antiques Fair** and the **Brewster Home Tour**. Many antiques dealers show their treasures for this annual event, which takes place the last weekend in June. The windimill is also open for the event. Call ☎ 508-896-7389 for information.

The Cape Cod Museum of Natural History sponsors a **home tour** on a select Saturday in late June. This is a chance to see homes that would not otherwise be open to the public. Refreshments are served. Call the museum at ☎ 508-896-3867 for further details.

July

The Fourth of July, **Independence Day**, in Provincetown is celebrated with a bang. There's a day-time parade and evening fireworks over the harbor. In Wellfleet the Independence Day Parade is considered one of the area's best shows. The town hosts a slew of other fun functions throughout the day. Call the Chamber of Commerce at ☎ 508-349-2510 for further details.

Fourth of July celebrations in Orleans include a parade down Main Street in the morning. Call the Chamber of Commerce at ☎ 508-255-1386 for further details.

August

In mid-August, the Provincetown Business Guild hosts a "**Carnival**," celebrating the gay lifestyle. This week-long affair includes such events as a Carnival Ball, Dixie Drag Extravaganza and more. Call ☎ 508-487-2313 for more information.

Also in Provincetown, enjoy the **Annual Benefit Auction**, with proceeds from the auction donated to the Fine Arts Work Center. Monies collected help support the fellowship program. Call ☎ 508-487-9960 for further details.

In Orleans, the **Pops in the Park** series of concerts is held each August in Eldredge Park. It features the Cape Cod Symphony Orchestra. ☎ 508-255-1386.

Music, art and concerts by the Chatham Corale are all part of the **Chatham Festival of the Arts**, taking place mid-month. The event is held at the Windmill in Chase Park. Call ☎ 508-945-5911 for further details.

September

Eastham's **Windmill Weekend** pays homage to the windmill. This celebration features a parade, a crafts show and more. Held the first weekend after Labor Day. Call ☎ 508-255-3444 for more information.

The Cape Cod Museum of Natural History sponsors an **Annual Bird Carvers Festival** in Brewster on the third weekend in September. For more information, ☎ 508-896-3867.

The Harwich **Cranberry Harvest Festival** is a very popular event which pays homage to the tasty and beautiful cranberry. This 10-day annual event includes a parade, Western jamboree, parade, fireworks and more. Call ☎ 508-430-2811 for further details.

The annual **Fall For Orleans Festival** is held the last weekend in September. Enjoy concerts, an antique car show, hayrides, sidewalk sales, a fashion show and more. Call ☎ 508-255-1386 for additional information.

November

Chatham By the Sea kicks off the holiday season in late November and sponsors events throughout the following month. These include a holiday dance, the arrival of Santa and more. Call ☎ 508-945-1122 for a list of events.

Holiday celebrating begins early in neighboring Orleans. Santa won't be riding a sleigh; instead he'll be taking children on hayrides. **Christmas is Orleans** also includes a candlelight stroll, tree decorating and a carol for good cheer. Call ☎ 508-255-1386.

December

Eastham Holiday Festival includes Santa's arrival by helicopter, ice sculptures, a chowder festival and more. Call ☎ 508-255-3444.

The annual **Lighting of the Monument** is Provincetown's homage to Christmas. Over 5,000 lights are draped from the Pilgrim's Monument, making it visible for miles.

First Night is celebrated throughout the Cape. This New Year's Eve event is become increasingly popular. Many of the towns sponsor dances, concerts, theatrical productions and more.

 Outdoor Fun

Forests, Parks & Preserves

The **Cape Cod National Seashore** is a 27,000-acre tract of land encompassing parts of Chatham, Orleans, Eastham, Wellfleet, Truro and Provincetown. The National Seashore was created during the Kennedy Adminsistration in 1961. Its main purpose is to preserve the stunning beauty of the Cape. You'll find hiking, fishing, swimming, horseback riding and biking here. The Cape Cod National Seashore Headquarters is located in South Wellfleet and is open year-round. Call ☎ 508-349-3785

The **Province Lands Trail** offers more than five miles of trails through sand dunes, marsh lands, woods and ponds. The wide expanse of sea will take your breath away, as will the view of the distant Boston skyline on clear days.

In Wellfleet, the four-mile **Great Island Trail** wanders through marsh, dunes, beach and meadows. Take Chequessett Neck Road to its end.

The short **Cranberry Bog Trail** in Truro offers conducted tours, giving you the opportunity to learn more about the wildlife and the Cape's vegetation. It focuses on the secret life of cranberries.

The Massachusetts Audobon Society offers trips, guided walks and tours through 1,000 acres of moors, salt marsh, beach, forest, ponds, tidal pools and more at the **Wellfleet Bay Wildlife Sanctuary**. Located in South Wellfleet, off Route 6. Call ☎ 508-349-2615.

The **Nickerson State Park** has it all: camping, biking, fishing, swimming, horseback riding and hiking. Located off Route 6A in Brewster, the park includes acres of forests, ponds and trails. Call ☎ 508-896-3491 for further details.

Chatham's **Monomoy National Wildlife Refuge** is rich with seafaring wildlife. This 2,750-acre preserve includes the Monomoy Islands. Certain areas are off-limits in an attempt to insure the safety of the birds nesting here. The area is wonderfully private, offering sand and sea, marshes, freshwater ponds and seashore plants and berries.

Harwich has its share of conservation areas, including 245 acres of land at **Herring Run**, off Bell's Neck Road. Nature lovers will also enjoy **Hawks Neck Pond**, which covers 44 acres of land (located at Hawks Neck Pond and Oliver's Pond).

Bicylcing

The **Cape Cod Rail Trail** offers 25 miles of path through and around forests, marshes, ponds and cranberry bogs. It runs from South Dennis to Wellfleet. Call ☎ 508-896-3491 for more information.

In Provincetown, explore the eight-mile **Province Land Bike Trail** connecting Herring Cove Beach, Race Point Beach and the Province Land 's Visitor Center. Call ☎ 508-487-1256.

Wonderful country lanes abound off many of the main roads. However, bicycle at your own risk on any of the major roads. Be sure to wear a helmet and watch out for approaching vehicles.

Beaches

The following beach chart shows what's offered at each beach on the Outer Cape.

	Admission Charge	Bath House	Beach Sticker Reqd.	Freshwater Beach	Parking Fee	Rest Rooms	Snack Bar
BREWSTER							
Breakwater Beach, Breakwater Rd.			*		*	*	
Crosby Landing, Crosby Ln.			*		*	*	
Ellis Landing, Ellis Landing Rd.			*		*	*	
Flax Pond, Nickerson State Park				*			
Linnell's Landing, Linnell Rd.			*		*	*	
Long Pond, Pine Rd.			*	*		*	
Paine's Creek Beach, Paine's Creek Rd.			*		*		
Robbins Hill Beach, Off Lowell Rd.			*		*	*	
Saint's Landing, Off Lower Rd.			*		*	*	
Schoolhouse Pond, Off Rte. 6A			*				
Sheep Pond, Off Rte. 124, Fisherman's landing			*	*		*	
Slough Pond, Pine Rd.			*	*			
Walker's Pond, Pine Rd.			*	*			
ORLEANS							
Nauset Beach, Off Rte. 28 or 6A		*			*	*	*
Pilgrim Lake, Off Monument Rd.				*		*	
PROVINCETOWN							
Herring Cove, At the end of Rte. 6A		*			*	*	*
Race Point, Off Rte. 6		*			*	*	
EASTHAM							
Campground Beach, Off Massasoit rd.	*				*	*	
Coast Guard Beach, Off Rte. 6		*			*	*	
Cooks Brook Beach, Cape Cod Bay					*	*	
First Encounter Beach, Cape Cod Bay					*	*	
Great Pond Beach, Great Pond Rd.				*	*		
Herring Pond, West side of Rte. 6				*	*	*	
Nauset Light Beach, Off Rte. 6	*	*			*	*	
Sunken Meadow Beach, Off Rte. 6					*		
Thumpertown Beach, Bayside	*		*		*	*	
Wiley Park Beach, Off Herring Brook Rd.				*	*	*	
TRURO							
Ballston Beach, Pamet Rd.			*			*	
Coast Guard Beach, Coast Guard Rd.			*			*	
Corn Hill Beach, Corn Hill Rd.	*		*			*	
Fisher Beach, Fisher Rd.			*				
Great Hollow Beach, Great Hollow Rd.			*			*	
Head of Meadow, Head of Meadow Rd.	*					*	
Longnook Beach, Longnook Rd.			*			*	
Ryder Beach, Ryder Rd.			*				
WELLFLEET							
Cahoon Hollow Beach, Off Ocean View Dr.			*	*			
Marconi Beach, So. Wellfleet		*			*	*	
White Crest Beach, Off Ocean View Dr.					*	*	

Recreation

Tennis

Provincetown Tennis Club, 286 Bradford Street, Provincetown, ☎ 508-487-9574.

Bissell's Tennis Court, Bradford Street, Provincetown, ☎ 508-487-9512.

Oliver Tennis Courts, Route 6, Wellfleet, ☎ 508-349-3330.

Norsemen Athletic Club, Route 6, Eastham, ☎ 508-255-6370.

Bamburgh House Tennis Club, Off Route 6A, Brewster, ☎ 508-896-5023.

Queen Anne Tennis, 70 Queen Anne Road, Chatham, ☎ 508-945-4726.

Golf

Eastward Ho Country Club, 325 Fox Hill Road, Chatham, ☎ 508-945-0003.

Oyster Harbor Club, Inc., 170 Grant Island, Osterville, ☎ 508-428-3131.

Cranberry Valley Golf Course, 183 Oak Street, Harwich, ☎ 508-430-7560.

Blue Rock Par 3 Golf Course, Off High Bank Road, South Yarmouth, ☎ 508-398-9295.

Captain Golf Course, 1000 Freeman's Way, Brewster, ☎ 508-896-5100.

Chatham Seaside Links, 209 Seaview, Chatham, ☎ 508-945-4774.

Chequessett Yacht and Country Club, Chequessett Neck Road, Wellfleet, ☎ 508-349-3704.

Harwich Port Golf Club, Forest, Harwich Port, ☎ 508-432-0250.

Highland Golf Club House, Highland Road, Truro, ☎ 508-487-9201.

Kings Way Golf Club, 64 Kings Circuit, Yarmouth, ☎ 508-362-8870.

Ocean Edge Golf Course, Ocean Edge, Route 6A, Brewster, ☎ 508-896-5911.

Boating

Flyer's Boat Rental (sailing, sea kayaks, power boat rentals and lessons), 131 A Commercial Avenue, Provincetown, ☎ 508-487-0898. (Also offers hourly shuttle service to Long Point.)

Schooner Hindu (sailing excursions), MacMillam Wharf, Provincetown, ☎ 800-296-4544.

Portuguese Princess Whale Watch, 70 Shank Painter Road, Provincetown, ☎ 508-487-2651 or 800-442-3188.

Dolphin Fleet of Provincetown Whale Watch, MacMillam Wharf, Provincetown, ☎ 508-349-1900 or 800-826-9300. http://www.whalewatch.com.

Wellfleet Marine Corp. (sailing and fishing rentals), Town Pier, Wellfleet, ☎ 508-349-2233.

 **Entertainment**

Movie Theaters

New Art Cinema, 214 Commercial Avenue, Provincetown, ☎ 508-487-9222.

Interstate Harwich Cinema, 181 Route 137, Harwich, ☎ 508-430-1160.

Wellfleet Drive-In Theater and Cinemas, Route 6, Wellfleet, ☎ 508-349-2520.

Performing Arts

Provincetown

Provincetown Repertory Theatre (contemporary theater), 336 Commercial Avenue, Provincetown, ☎ 508-487-0600.

Provincetown Theatre Company (new and classic theater), 391 Commercial Street, ☎ 508-487-8673.

The Muse Series, sponsored by the Provincetown Playhouse, and the **Beach Plum Music Series** (folk and jazz performances) take place at the Town Hall and the Universalist Meeting House. Consult local newspaper for listing of events.

Wellfleet

Wellfleet Harbor Actors Theater - WHAT (contemporary, avant-garde), Kendrick Avenue, ☎ 508-3496835.

Brewster

Cape Cod Repertory Theatre (indoor and outdoor theaters, contemporary theatrical offerings), Route 6A, Brewster, ☎ 508-896-6140.

Chatham

The Chatham Drama Guild (contemporary theater), 134 Crowell Road, Chatham, ☎ 508-945-3563.

Monomoy Theatre (musicals, classics, dramas), Main Street, Chatham, ☎ 508-945-1589.

Orleans

Academy of Performing Arts, 120 Main Street, Orleans, ☎ 508-255-1963.

Nightlife

Chatham

Wequassett Inn (piano lounge), Pleasant Bay Road, ☎ 508-432-5400.

Chatham Sands (dancing to the oldies-but-goodies), Route 28, ☎ 508-945-4424.

Upstairs at Christian's (piano bar), 443 Main Street, ☎ 508-945-3362.

The Chatham Bar's Inn (varied music and dance), Shore Road, ☎ 508-945-0096.

Northport Seafood House (varied venues), 323 Route 28, ☎ 508-945-9217.

Brewster

The Reef Café (Rhythm and Blues, top 40's bands), 1 Village Drive, ☎ 508-896-7167.

Harwich

Bishop's Terrace (concert pianist Ken Manzer), Route 28, West Harwich, ☎ 508-432-0253.

Goucho's (jazz and the blues), 403 Lower County Road, Harwich Port, ☎ 508-432-7768.

Orleans

Off the Bay Café (Broadway and Gershwin), 28 Main Street, ☎ 508-255-5505.

Academy of Performing Arts (Friday evening ballroom dancing), Town Hall Annex, ☎ 508-255-5510.

Land Ho! (varied venues), Route 6A, ☎ 508-255-5165.

Eastham

First Encounter Coffee House (small concerts), Samoset Road, ☎ 508-255-5438.

Wellfleet

The Tavern Room at the Inn at Duck Creeke (jazz), E. Main Street, ☎ 508-349-7369.

Provincetown

Club Euro (jazz, funk, reggae), 258 Commercial Street, ☎ 508-487-2505.

Atlantic House (popular gay bar with either live music or a deejay), 4 Masonic Place, ☎ 508-487-3821.

Pied Piper (lesbian dance club), 193 Commercial Street, ☎ 508-487-1527.

Reaching The Outer Cape

By Car

From New York: Take I-95 through Connecticut to Rhode Island. From Providence, take I-195 East. At Bourne, take Route 25 East (I-195 South) over the Bourne Bridge to Route 28 South to Route 6.

From Boston: Take Route 3 (to the Sagamore Bridge) to Route 6 or Route 6A. Route 6 is faster; Route 6A, more beautiful.

By Air

The closest ariport is **Hyannis**. Airlines serving the area include: **Cape Air**, with service from Boston to Hyannis ☎ 800-352-0714; and **US Air Express**, which flies to Hyannis from Nantucket, New York and Washington D.C. (seasonal), ☎ 800-428-4322.

By Bus

Plymouth and Brockton Bus Line: Service from Logan Airport and South Station in Boston to Sagamore, Barnstable and Hyannis with connecting buses to the Outer Cape.

By Ferry

Bay State Cruises: A three-hour ferry ride connecting Boston to Provincetown. From the Cape, ☎ 508-487-9284; in Boston, ☎ 617-723-7800.

Freedom Cruise Line: Offering passanger service from Harwich Port to Nantucket Island. The 1½-hour cruise operates from May through October. ☎ 508-432-8999.

For More Information

Cape Cod Chamber of Commerce, ☎ 508-362-3225.

Chatham Chamber of Commerce, ☎ 508-945-0342.

Eastham Chamber of Commerce, ☎ 508-255-3444.

Harwich Chamber of Commerce, ☎ 508-432-1600.

Orleans Chamber of Commerce, ☎ 508-255-1386.

Truro Chamber of Commerce, ☎ 508-487-1288.

Wellfleet Chamber of Commerce, ☎ 508-349-2510.

Provincetown Chamber of Commerce, ☎ 508-487-3424.

Nantucket

Whenever I find myself growing grim about the mouth; whenever it is a damp drizzly November in my soul; whenever I find myself involuntarily pausing before coffin warehouses, and bringing up the rears of every funeral I meet; and especially when my hopes get an upper hand of me, that it requires a strong moral principle to prevent me from deliberately stepping into the street and methodically knocking people's hats off, then I account it is high time to get to the sea as soon as I can. This is my substitute for pistol and ball. With a philosophical flourish Cato throws himself upon his sword; I quietly take to the ship. There is nothing surprising in this. If they but knew it, almost all men in their degree, some time or another, cherish very nearly the same feelings toward the ocean with me.

~ Herman Melville, *Moby Dick*, 1819-1891

Nantucket is a very special place, a remote island away from mainland of America It has the beauty of a 19th-century town and is the perfect spot for romantics to enjoy the holiday of a lifetime.

Nantucket has several names. The original Indian inhabitants called it Nanticut, loosely translated as "faraway land." More recently it has been called the Little Grey Lady of the Sea after the weatherbeaten grey shingles covering many of the island's houses.

Thirty miles of sea separate Nantucket from the mainland. It's a three-hour ferry ride, an hour or more flight from Boston. The Island is about 14 miles long and 3½ miles wide. The terrain is relatively flat with long stretches of beach. Here you will find flora and fauna indigenous to the island: berries, bogs, salt marshes, ponds, birds, and fish. The town of Nantucket is a gem, adorned by cobblestone streets, 19th-century buildings

and old-fashioned street lamps. The island was designated as a National Historical District in 1955.

The island has several other villages besides Nantucket. To the east are Siasconset and Wauwinet, which are particularly pretty and have several romantic lodging possibilities. The southern portion of the island is less populated with large stretches of beach. To the west is Madaket, also quite rural. The Madaket area is known for its moors that were formerly used for raising sheep.

A huge amount of effort has been put into maintaining Nantucket's beauty. You won't find traffic lights. About a third of the land is protected by the Nantucket Conservation Foundation, established in 1963. Building codes have been enacted, with preservation being foremost in the minds of the local residents.

The original Nantucket residents were the Wampanoag Indians, who for centuries lived here in relative peace and harmony. The first white settlers were Quakers, who came in the late 17th century to escape religious persecution.

It was the whaling industry that put Nantucket on the map. In the early 1900s, Nantucket was considered the whaling capital of the world. During this time many of the houses and commercial buildings you see today were built. Whaling legends and lore continue to fascinate visitors to the island.

Like the rest of the region, Nantucket was hit hard when the whaling days came to an end. The Great Fire of 1846 destroyed about a third of the town of Nantucket. It took a while for the island to recuperate, but by the later part of the 19th century, Nantucket began to transform itself into a resort. For the past century, it has been a mecca for weary city-dwellers looking for a respite from their busy days.

D.M. BLACKBURN

Romantic Hotels & Inns

✦ The Jared Coffin House

Entering the Jared Coffin House is a treat. The main building is a three-story brick mansion built in 1845 by a wealthy shipowner. The sitting room features authentic period furnishings with a black marble fireplace, black-and-white tile checkerboard flooring, and Oriental carpeting. Tables and chairs are set up for a game of cards in the game room, which also has a black marble fireplace and an ornate antique mirror hanging from the mantel. Room 301, the Crewel Room, has a tapestry canopy bed and sofa alongside a white marble fireplace. Room 303 is another favorite of lovers, featuring a high ceiling and canopy bed with carved pineapple bedposts made of dark wood.

DONNA M. BLACKBURN

The lace curtains complement the dogwood design wallpaper with light pink and green details on a cream-colored background. From every room are views of the town streets and gardens.

The hotel's restaurant is a long-time favorite for visitors and locals alike, with Victorian-era furniture and light salmon wallpaper. The dark wood-paneled pub in the basement is typical of a whaling-era establishment, featuring folk art pieces and gaslight fixtures. A pleasant and very romantic outdoor café offers lunch or dinner Sit out here and admire the cascading floral growth and ivy on the brick walls. Open year-round.

The Jared Coffin House
29 Broad Street
P.O. Box 1580
Nantucket, MA 02554
☎ 508-228-2400 or 800-248-2405
Fax 508-228-8549
E-mail Jchouse@nantucket.net
www.nantucket.net/lodging/jchouse
$$$

The Ship's Inn

The Ship's Inn has plenty of charm. The rooms are light and airy with high ceilings and antique furnishings. The building was constructed in 1831 as a private residence for sea captain Obed Starbuck; the 10 guest rooms are named after his ships. The innkeepers are proud of the building's heritage, particularly because it was the birthplace of the famous abolitionist Lucretia Mott.

Choose from such guest quarters as the Success Room, featuring a light unfinished wood canopied bed and a wonderfully playful light green wallpaper. Or request the Huntress Room, with its nouveau country motif.

The inn's lovely and popular restaurant is an intimate place. The low ceiling, large brick fireplace, authentic sideboards, and old ship models set the mood.

A continental breakfast is served daily for guests. Open from April through October.

The Ships Inn
13 Fair Street
Nantucket, MA 02554
☎ *508-228-0040*
$$$

The House of the Seven Gables

This unique establishment has tastefully decorated rooms, several with views of the town and harbor. The downstairs rooms are quite formal, with dark wood period piece furnishings and dark red carpeting. In contrast, the guest rooms have lighter color combinations. The third-floor, light blue Honeymoon Suite has a bed nestled romantically under the eaves. The suite's sitting room offers harbor views.

Get treated to breakfast in bed. Your chambermaid will present you each day with a tray set with cut flowers, freshly prepared baked goods, juice, coffee, and tea.

The House of the Seven Gables
32 Cliff Road
Nantucket, MA 02554
☎ *508-228-4796*

❦ The Carlisle House Inn

There's something very romantic about the Carlisle House Inn. The Sitting Room is painted Colonial blue and has antique furnishings. The whaling-era painting aboves the mantel gives the room a special nautical air.

The 14 guest rooms are nicely decorated. The master bedrooms have canopied beds and working fireplaces. Many have views of the town and harbor. Room one receives the most requests, as it features a four-poster bed and wood panel fireplace, with a view of the garden. Romantics will also enjoy room 20, which has deep rose-colored walls, drapery, and upholstery. The room offers great views of the town and the sea. The two-room suite, Room 24, is beautifully decorated with a queen-size four-poster bed and fireplace offset by dark green and salmon-colored wallpaper.

Continental breakfast is served daily in the cheerful breakfast nook or outdoors in the garden (weather permitting).

DONNA M. BLACKBURN

The Carlisle House
26 North Water Street
Nantucket, MA 02554
☎ *508-228-0720*

The Cobblestone Inn

The Cobblestone combines the best of the old and new. The house was built in 1725, but much of the interior has been refurbished with newly painted white walls, natural light wood accents, and exposed beams.

The rooms are completely private; No room has a common wall with another. The third-floor suite is lovely, featuring a handmade quilt, lace curtains and a wonderful view of Nantucket and the harbor. A ground-floor room in the back of the inn has its own deck, lightly colored walls, swag drapes, a private bath, and large bed, making it a very romantic hideaway. Yet another room features a dark wood four-poster bed, exposed wood, and a Dutch-tiled fireplace. The innkeepers are quite friendly.

The Cobblestone Inn
5 Ash Street
Nantucket, MA 02554
☎ *508-288-1987*
$$$

✈ The Cliff Lodge

I fell in love with this place the moment I walked inside. It's French country decor is so light and airy, it couldn't be more romantic. Light blue-and-white striped wallpaper, handmade quilts, French wicker furnishings and a view of the harbor make the room. What more can you ask for? Climb the steep stairs to the widow's walk, which offers 360° view of the town, sea and surrounding area. The gardens are open for a leisurely afternoon stroll. Continental breakfast is served on the patio in the garden.

DONNA M. BLACKBURN

Cliff Lodge
9 Cliff Road
Nantucket, MA 02554
☎ *508-228-9480*
$$$

The Century House

A charming place to stay. The sitting room is cozy with light blue and white striped wallpaper contrasting with dark authentic period furniture. Innkeepers Gerry Connick and Jean Heron are great lovers of art and there are plenty of original works hanging on the walls. Of special interest is a painting of the house by Richard French. (After staying here in 1989, he was inspired to paint a watercolor of the house). The guest rooms are named for flowers and berries and decorated in country style, with white batiste curtains and furniture painted in light colors. Several of the front rooms have nice views of the area.

Enjoy a quiet moment in the secluded courtyard in back. You can't go wrong here. Open year-round.

The Century Inn
10 Cliff Road
P.O. Box 603
Nantucket, MA 02554
☎ *508-228-0530*
E-mail CenturyBnB@aol.com
www.centuryhouse.com
$$$

The Harbor House

Looking for a resort-style vacation which still qualifies as a romantic holiday? Then go no farther than the Harbor House. Choose from such accommodations as a guest room in the Main Hotel, a Garden Cottage or the Springfield House. Or consider a townhouse room located in one of six buildings resembling early Nantucket homes. The Sherburne Cottage is a fully equipped three-bedroom home. The hotel has tennis courts and an outdoor pool for guests only. The resort's restaurant, The Hearth, is a favorite spot for islanders and visitors alike. Open from April until December.

The Harbor House, A Colony Resort
South Beach Street
P.O. Box 1139
☎ *800-ISLANDS; hotel* ☎ *508-228-1500*
$$$$

The White Elephant and The Breakers

Sister resort to the Harbor House, the White Elephant and the Breakers offers its guests all of the amenities you have come to expect at a resort. Located on the harbor, many of the rooms have spectacular views. The harborside pool is the perfect place to spend the afternoon sipping a soda or lemonade, reading a novel and taking dips to cool off. Rooms range from single rooms to one- , two- and three-bedroom cottages. The hotel's restaurant, the Brant Point Grill, offers indoor and outdoor terrace seating. Open from May until October.

The White Elephant & The Breakers
Easton Street
P.O. Box 1139
Nantucket, MA 02554
☎ *508-228-2500 or 800-ISLANDS*
Fax 508-325-1195
$$$$

The Easton House

It was innkeeper Judith Ross' friendliness that first led us to believe that we had arrived at a very special place. She and her husband Cyril will spread their good cheer and are commited to making your stay a happy one.

The inn was built in 1812 and has maintained much of its original charm. The sitting room is has wood paneling with lace curtains and period piece furnishings. On the first floor you will find a lovely authentic antique room with a four-poster canopy bed with a handmade quilt featuring detailed lace. The wood paneling, quaint iron fireplace, lace curtains, and corner bathroom give this room its romantic flair.

Lovers seeking privacy should consider the Garden Cottage. It's bright and roomy, decorated with country-style furnishings and chintz rose draperies. A fully equipped kitchen allows guests to stay sequestered in the back. A perfect honeymoon retreat!

A complimentary full continental breakfast is served daily. Open year-round.

The Easton House
17 North Water Street
Box 1033
Nantucket, MA 02554
☎ *508-228-2759*
$$$

The Nantucket Landfall

This waterfront inn has a lovely front garden and large porch. Upon entering, you'll find a cozy the sitting room with a fireplace and library. Its nautical theme is perfect for a Nantucket vacation.

The Nantucket Landfall has a nice fresh feel to it. The guest rooms are quaint, nicely decorated with antiques and handmade quilts and pillow shams. For romantics, I suggest the Snuggery, a charming antique-filled cottage behind the main house. Another room for lovers is the Essex, in the main house. It has a canopied double bed and a sitting room overlooking the harbor.

The inn offers a daily continental breakfast featuring home-baked specialties. Open year-round.

The Nantucket Landfall
Four Harborview Way
Nantucket, MA 02554
☎ *508-228-0500*
$$$

Nantucket

✈ Wauwinet Inn

The Wauwinet overlooks the sea and features a sweeping lawn leading down to a private beach. Here you will find 25 rooms and five individual cottages decorated with pine antiques that lend a country/beach feeling. Several of the rooms have ocean views.

The inn has many activities available for guests, including tennis, biking, and sailing. A croquet game may well be taking place on the lawn, and you can also play a game of chess with life-size wooden chess pieces on the large chessboard.

DONNA M. BLACKBURN

The inn schedules Land Rover tours of the Great Pond Reserve and there's a shuttle service from the ferry dock in the town of Nantucket.

The restaurant, Toppers, is famous and well-deserving of its popularity. It's a perfect place for romantics to enjoy each other and the gastronomical delights placed upon the table.

Wauwinet Inn
Wauwinet Road
Box 2580
Nantucket, MA 02584
☎ *508-228-6715 or 800-426-8718*
Fax 508-228-6712
$$$$

🏹 The Summer House

Located across from the Siasconset Beach, the rose-covered cottages of the Summer House offer a secluded getaway for lovers. Decorated in a combination of beach and country English styles, there's plenty of Laura Ashley and stripped pine antique furnishings. Some of the guest rooms have fireplaces. Ask for one with a marble bath and whirlpool. Lunch at the poolside café is a must, as is dining at the Summer House's restaurant, considered to be one of the best on the island. Open from June through October.

The Summer House
Ocean Avenue
Box 880
Siasconset, MA 02564
☎ *508-257-4577*
Fax 508-257-4590
$$$$

DONNA M. BLACKBURN

Restaurants

The Chanticleer

Located in Siasconset, this restaurant has earned its reputation for fine dining because owner/chef Jean-Charles Berruet knows his stuff. Serving both lunch and dinner, the dining rooms are quite formal. If you want something more casual, ask to be seated in the Rose Garden. The restaurant serves nouvelle cuisine and classic seafood.

> *The Chanticleer*
> *9 New Street*
> ☎ *508-257-6231 or 508-257-9756*
> *$$$$*

Toppers

Another quintessential Nantucket dining experience, Toppers is located at the Wauwinet Inn. This formal and elegant restaurant offers a nice variety of seafood specialties such as pan-seared sea scallops with lobster risotto. Sunday brunch here has been a Nantucket favorite for years. Serving lunch and dinner throughout the season, reservations are needed.

> *Toppers at the Wauwinet Inn*
> ☎ *508-228-8768*
> *$$$$*

The Summer House

This restaurant is located on the South Bluff of Siasconset with panoramic views of the Atlantic. It offers a romantic setting, and you can choose to dine in the formal dining room with dark green walls and white wicker furniture or by the pool, which offers a backdrop of the Atlantic. The entrées are to die for, including such specialties as grilled lobster over warm marinated new potato and haricots vert with black truffle sauce, or roast rack of lamb with a hazelnut crust served with baby spinach and beet risotto. Reservations are recommended.

The Summer House
Ocean Avenue
Siasconset
☎ *508-257-9976*
$$$$

The Second Story

This intimate second-story restaurant has hand-painted walls and flickering candlelight at the tables. The menu is wonderfully eclectic, with such entrées as salmon with ginger and garlic sauce or steak with port sauce and garlic mashed potatoes.

The Second Story
1 South Beach Street
☎ *508-228-3471*
$$$

India House

The three small dining rooms which comprise this restaurant have low, beamed ceilings and are decorated in Colonial style. Serving continental and nouvelle American specialties, menu selections include an assortment of fresh seafood and meat dishes. The restaurant is housed in a building that was formerly a private residence. The house was built in 1803. An outdoor dining area is open during the summer months. The restaurant also serves a Sunday brunch.

The India House
37 India Street
☎ *508-228-9043*
$$$$

The Ship's Inn Restaurant

Intimacy reigns at this cozy candlelit restaurant just a short walk from downtown. Serving California-French cuisine, chef/owner Mark Gottwald's culinary experiences include graduating from La Varenne in Paris and apprenticeships at Spago's and Le Cirque. Dinner entrées include duck crêpe with roasted plum sauce and medallions of Maine lobster with leek.

The Ship's Inn
13 Fair Street
☎ *508-228-0040*
$$$$

The Jared Coffin House

Dine in Victorian elegance at the Jared Coffin Inn. The beautifully restored main dining room with soft peach wallpaper and a baby grand piano has a wonderful old feeling to it. Or consider dining in the downstairs pub, also beautifully restored, with dark wood paneling (it feels as though you've traveled back in time by a century). The outdoor café is also a treat, with flowers cascading down the walls. Menu selection include a variety of fresh seafood, fowl, and meat dishes. Enjoy the seafood buffet served on Wednesdays and Sundays throughout the summer. A Sunday brunch is offered throughout the year.

The Jared Coffin House
29 Broad Street
☎ *508-228-2400*
$$$$

De Marco

De Marco has earned a reputation for its fine Northern Italian cuisine. Located in downtown Nantucket, this two-story, 19th-century restaurant has charm and style. The menu changes frequently, but the emphasis is always on fresh pastas, meats, and seafood. Entrées include such items as *capellini alla reggie con vongole* (steamed tender clams in a broth of vermouth, garlic, vegetables, and fresh herbs over angel hair pasta) and *osso bucco d'agnello con verdure glasate* (braised tender lamb in white wine, garlic, and rosemary over glazed root vegetables and barley risotto). Reservations are recommended.

DeMarco
9 India Street
☎ *508-228-1836*
$$$$

Other Eateries

Café Expresso is a coffee house with style, a place to relax after a day of shopping or touring. There's an assortment of sandwiches, pastries, and desserts, and a number of coffee flavors to choose from. Located in downtown Nantucket, you can't miss it. *Café Expresso, 40 Main Street,* ☎ *508-228-6930. $*

Remember the good old days when pharmacies had lunch counters to soothe the soul? If you want take a trek back to an earlier era, the **Nantucket Pharmacy's** lunch counter is just the place. *Nantucket Pharmacy, 45 Main Street,* ☎ *508-228-0180. $*

Provisions sandwich shop, located on Straight Wharf, gets all sorts of good press. It serves breakfast and lunch and also offers picnic lunches if you're heading for the beach. *Provisions, Straight Wharf,* ☎ *508-228-3258. $*

Touring The Town Of Nantucket

Nantucket has a rich history and island locals are very proud of it. The **Museum of Nantucket History**, located at Straight Wharf, provides a comprehensive overview of the island's history. Of particular note is the 13-foot-tall diorama showing the layout of the town before the Great Fire of 1846. An excellent collection of early photographs depicting Nantucket throughout history is quite impressive. Don't miss the live demonstrations of early island crafts.

❦

Cobblestones

The cobblestone streets in downtown Nantucket give the town a special allure. The stones were brought to the island as ballast on returning ships. Although the cobblestones are quite beautiful, they were placed on Nantucket's streets for utilitarian purposes. They were primarily used to prevent the wheels of carts filled with whale oil from sinking into the dirt.

❦

One of the oldest libraries in the nation, the **Antheum** stands majestically at the corner of India and Oak streets. The windowless facade, framed by Ionic columns, is an excellent example of Greek Revival architecture. Built in 1847, the library was closed for renovations in 1996, but re-opened recently.

The **Nantucket Historical Society** (NHA) maintains 11 historical sites and offers tours throughout the summer. Call ☎ 508-228-0665 for information regarding tours, lectures, and other events. Tours will allow you access to the following places:

The **Fire-Hose Cart House** features a collection of 19th-century fire-fighting equipment. Built in 1886, the house is the last remaining example of a neighborhood fire station. Located on Gardner Street.

The **Quaker Meeting House** on Fair Street is the home to the **Fair Street Museum**, housing much of the NHA's collection of Nantucket artifacts. The 1838 building was originally a Friends School but was converted to a meeting house in 1864. Quaker services continue to be held here.

The elegance of Greek Revival architecture is evident at the **Hawden House**, 96 Main Street. Built by Frederick Brown Coleman in 1844 and later owned by William Hawden, a whale oil magnate, the house has been furnished and decorated with items from the mid-19th century.

The oldest house on the island is the **Jethro Coffin House** on Sunset Hill. It was built in 1686. Tours are given daily during the summer season.

An excellent example of Colonial Revival period architecture is the **Macy-Christian House** at Liberty Street and Walnut Lane.

The **Vestal Street Jail** (the Old Gaol) was built in 1805 and is one of the oldest jails in the United States. Jail conditions were pretty harsh back then. The jail offered relatively grim accommodations with rough plank bunks, open privies, and iron-grated windows.

The **Old Mill** on Prospect Street was built in 1746. This working mill continues to grind corn. You can view a demonstration of the wooden gears that harness the wind to power the mill.

Nantucket's whaling history is explored at the **Whaling Museum** on Broad Street. Here you will learn everything you ever wanted to know about Nantucket's glorious whaling past. Maintained by the NHA (Nantucket Historical Society), the museum features a 43-foot finback whale skeleton, a whale-boat, ship models, nautical tools, and ship's logs. Allow yourself some time to visit the scrimshaw room, which has pieces of incredible beauty and detail.

The history of Nantucket has been chronicled at **The Peter Foulger Museum**. Here you will find the Nantucket Historical Association's "Away Off Shore" exhibition. Nantucket's whaling history, ship logs, and genealogical charts are also on display. For more information call the NHA at ☎ 508-228-1655.

Nantucket native Maria Mitchell was the first American to discover a telescopic comet. In 1865 she became the first female professor of astronomy at Vassar College. The Maria Mitchell Association has several sites on the island, including the following:

The Mitchell House, Maria Mitchell's birthplace, is open to the public. Furnished in 19th-century Quaker tradition, the house was built in 1790. Located at 1 Vestal Street. Call ☎ 508-228-9198 for tour schedule.

Next door (at 2 Vestal Street) you will find the **Science Library**, which is also open to the public throughout the summer.

The **Nantucket Aquarium** at 28 Washington Street offers several collecting trips throughout the summer months and has saltwater and freshwater tanks. Call ☎ 508-228-5387 for further details.

Discover the natural history of Nantucket at the **Hinchman House**. Here you will find displays of Nantucket flora and fauna. Join a group of other nature and birdwatching enthusiasts during one of their daily nature walks. Located at 7 Milk Street. Call ☎ 508-228-0898.

Discover the stars in all their glory at the **Observatory**, also on Milk Street. Several programs are offered throughout the summer, including children's science seminars and public telescope nights. Call ☎ 508-228-9273 for schedule information.

A walk down **Upper Main Street** is an absolute must. Here you will find a row of mansions built during Nantucket's golden whaling era. The **Three Bricks Mansions** were built by whaling merchant Joseph Starbuck for his sons in the 1830s. Located at 93-97 Upper Main Street, these private residences are wonderful examples of Greek Revival architecture.

The **First Congregational Church**, 62 Centre Street, was built in 1834. Also known as the Old North Church, the church's 120-foot steeple rises majestically. You can climb the 92 steps for a panoramic view of the island. The interior has its original old box pews, a seven-foot-wide chandelier, and a restored trompe l'oeil ceiling created by an Italian painter in 1850. Also of note is the 1809 **Unitarian Universalist Church** (also known as the South Church), which has a gold-domed spire. The town clock makes its home here, as does the bell, which has been ringing ever since it was brought here from Portugal in 1815.

Scrimshaw

The history of the making of scrimshaw cannot be overlooked in a romantic guidebook to this area. Years ago, during the whaling era, men left their loved ones at home for long periods of time while they searched the seas for whales. In order to pass the time, many of the men began carving whale ivory and whale bones to make beautiful gifts for their wives and girlfriends.

Another art form which came from the whaling era was the Sailor's Valentine, a three-dimensional decoration made of exotic shells collected from around the world. The shells were arranged in patterns, affixed to wood, and given to sweethearts. View the legacy of these art forms, now on display at several of the local museums.

DONNA M. BLACKBURN

Touring The Island Of Nantucket

The town of Nantucket may well be the hub of activity on the island, but to experience Nantucket at its most pristine, a visit to the towns of **Siasconset** (pronounced SKONset) and **Wauwinet** is well worth your while. Six miles southeast of the town of Nantucket, Siasconset has maintained much of its fishing village charm. Here you will find the small, colorful cottages, former fishing shacks turned into summer residences for the actors and actresses from New York who have been coming here since the early 1900s. The town of Siasconset consists of a post office, gas station, and several famous restaurants. Be sure to take a stroll away from Main Street down narrow lanes. Here you will find small dollhouse cottages with roses spilling from the roof.

On **Ocean Avenue** the spectacular movements of large rolling waves from the Atlantic will keep you spellbound. Large summer mansions now line this street.

On the northeast corner of Nantucket Island is Wauwinet, known for its summer beach houses and the historic Wauwinet Resort. Farther north, on the very tip of the island, is the Great Point Lighthouse. The area can be accessed only by foot or by four-wheel-drive vehicle. Nantucket wildlife find protection here as the land is watched over by the Nantucket Conservation Foundation.

The southern portion of the island is less populated but outdoor opportunities abound on its large stretches of beach. To the west is **Madaket**, a relatively rural area worth visiting. Here you will find the rolling fields and plains comprising the 300-acre **Sanford Farm**. This area is commonly referred to as "the moors."

Nantucket Lightship Baskets

More than likely, you'll fall in love with the intricate beauty of handwoven Nantucket lightship baskets. Now featured primarily in jewelry, the lightship baskets were originally made by the Nantucket Indians.

Annual Events

For information about any of the events listed below, ☎ 508-228-1700.

April

The Daffodil Festival is held at the end of April. The town goes wild with daffodil displays all over and many residents participate in a contest for the best display. An antique automobile parade, a Daffodil Ball, and a picnic in Siasconset are all part of the festivities.

May

Figawi Race: Held on Memorial Day weekend, this regatta from Hyannis to Nantucket has plenty of fanfare, including a clambake and a dance.

July

The **Fourth of July** brings something for everyone: a bike race, antique car parade, windsurfing regatta and, of course, fireworks.

Rose Sunday is sponsored by the Congregational Church on Centre Street. The church is decorated with thousands of roses and is a beautiful sight. Held on a selected Sunday in July.

August

The Chamber of Commerce sponsors a **Sandcastle Contest** on Jetties Beach.

December

Christmas Stroll: Nantucket goes all-out celebrating the Christmas season during the first weekend in December, when the streets are lined with Christmas trees decorated by the school children. Carolers stroll the streets, shops give samples of eggnog, hot cider and other yummy goodies associated with the season. Santa arrives around 4 o'clock in a horse-drawn carriage at the Pacific Bank, where he helps light the main Christmas tree (trees lining Main Street follow suit). A sight to see and a favorite event of both locals and vacationers.

 Outdoor Fun

Preserves, Forests & Parks

With over a third of the island protected from further development, the number of outdoor recreational spots are unlimited on Nantucket. Travel by foot, bus, bike, or automobile to experience Nantucket's natural wonders.

More than 200 acres of cranberry bogs are surrounded by conservation land at the **Milestone Bog** east of downtown Nantucket. Just north of here is the **Windswept Cranberry Bog**, another 205-acre parcel of land. Cranberries transform from their light pink color in early summer to bright red in early fall.

The small strip of land between Nantucket Harbor and Nantucket Sound is the **Coatue Wildlife Refuge**, a favorite fishing spot. The beaches, sand dunes, and salt marshes collectively known as the **Coskata Wildlife Refuge** are home to all sorts of seabirds, including egrets, marsh hawks, terns, herring gulls, and nesting osprey. The **Sesachacha Pond** also offers good birdwatching opportunities.

Enjoy the wide expanses of open moor and bog lands at **Altar Rock**, located near Wauwinet. On the south shore of the Island is **Miacomet Pond**. This freshwater pond, where you will find pond creatures, swans, snapping turtles, and ducks, is separated from the ocean by a narrow strip of land.

Take Surfside Road to Miacomet Road and the **Sanford Farm, Ram Pasture** and **The Woods**. These three areas combine to offer 900 acres of wetlands, forest, and grasslands. Several trails will lead you through the area. The 6½-mile walking trail passing Hummock Pond has interpretive markers for naturalists wanting to learn more about Nantucket's plants and wildlife. Access is available at the intersection of Madaket and Cliff roads.

The **Land Bank Walking Trail** on the western end of the island offers a three-quarter-mile walk through meadows, swamps, hawthorn grove and blueberry patches.

Nearby is **Eel Point**, another place for taking a stroll through Nantucket's natural wonders. This is a popular spot to watch the sunset. Or take a nature tour sponsored by the **Maria Mitchell Association**. Call ☎ 508-228-9198 for more information.

Nantucket

Beaches

BEACHES	Lifeguard	Food	Parking	Rest rooms
Children's Beach, Harbor View Way	*	*	*	*
Cisco Beach, Hummock Pond Rd.	*		*	
Dionis Beach, Nantucket Sound	*		*	*
Jetties Beach, North Beach St.	*	*	*	*
Madaket Beach, 5 miles from town	*		*	*
Surfside Beach,Surfside Rd.	*	*	*	*
Brandt Point, harbor entrance				
Francis St. Beach, Francis St.				*
Siasconset Beach,Ocean Ave.	*		*	

Recreation

Golf

Miacomet Golf Club, 12 W. Miacomet Road, ☎ 508-325-0333.

Siasconset Golf Club, Milestone Road, Siasconset, ☎ 508-257-6596.

Tennis

Brant Point Racquet Club, 48 N. Beach Street, ☎ 508-228-3700.

Jetties Beach Tennis Courts, 2 Bathing Beach Road, ☎ 508-325-5334.

Tristam's Landing Tennis Club, 440 Arkansas Avenue, Madaket, ☎ 508-228-4588.

Boating

Anna W II Harbor Cruises, Slip #12, Straight Wharf, ☎ 508-228-1444.

Christina Sailing Excursion, ☎ 508-325-4000.

Endeavor Sailing Excursions, Slip #15, Straight Wharf, ☎ 508-228-5585.

Force 5 Watersports, Jetties Beach, ☎ 508-228-5358.

Island Sails Charters, ☎ 508-325-0202.

Nantucket Boat Rentals, Roundabout, ☎ 508-325-1001.

Nantucket Harbor Sail, Petrel Landing, Swain's Wharf, ☎ 508-228-0424.

Nantucket Sailing Charters, ☎ 508-228-3464.

Nantucket Whale Boat Adventures, ☎ 508-228-5585.

Sea Nantucket Kayak Rentals, Washington Street Excursion, ☎ 508-228-7499.

Sparrow Yacht Charters, Slip # 18, Straight Wharf, ☎ 508-228-6029.

The Wauwinet Lady, Harbor launch float, Straight Wharf, ☎ 508-228-0145.

Sightseeing Tours

Adventure Tours of Nantucket, ☎ 508-228-1686.

All Points Tours, ☎ 508-325-5779.

Ara's Tours, ☎ 508-228-1951.

Barrett's Tours, ☎ 508-228-0174.

Betty's Tour, ☎ 508-228-5786.

BG's Tours, ☎ 508-325-1515.

Gail's Tours, ☎ 508-257-6557.

Grimes Tours, ☎ 508-228-9382.

Island Tours, Straight Wharf, ☎ 508-228-0334.

Trustees of Reservations Great Point Natural History Tours, ☎ 508-228-3559.

Entertainment

Movies

Dreamland, 19 Water Street, ☎ 508-228-5365.

Gaslight Theater, North Union Street, ☎ 508-228-4435.

Siasconset Casino Stage, New Street, Siasconset, ☎ 508-257-6585.

Plays & Concerts

Actor's Theatre of Nantucket at Gordon Folger Hotel on Easton Street, ☎ 508-228-6325. Professional summer theater.

Theatre Workshop of Nantucket, Bennett Hall, Box 1297, ☎ 508-228-4305. Amateur theater group, year-round performances.

Nantucket Short Play Festival. Call for schedule, ☎ 508-228-5002.

Band Concert, Harbor Square. Every night at 7 p.m. throughout July and August, at the gazebo.

Nantucket Chamber Music Center, 11 Centre Street, ☎ 508-228-3352.

Nantucket Musical Arts Society, ☎ 508-228-1287. Concerts throughout the summer.

Thursday Noonday Concerts, Unitarian Universalist Church, 11 Orange Street, ☎ 508-228-0738 or 508-228-2730.

Nightlife

The Regatta at the White Elephant (dancing, cabaret), Easton Street, ☎ 508-228-2500.

The Tap Room at the Jared Coffin House (piano), 29 Broad Street, ☎ 508-228-2400.

The Club Car (piano, sing along with Scott Olsen), 1 Main Street, ☎ 508-228-1101.

The Brotherhood (live music, six nights a week), 23 Broad Street.

The Box (popular music from the 1960s-1990s), ☎ 508-228-9717.

Chancellor's At The Point, Breeze Hotel (piano, nightly throughout the season), 71 Easton Street, ☎ 508-228-0313.

The Galley on Cliffside Beach, (jazz piano), Jefferson Avenue, ☎ 508-228-9641.

The House of Muse-Ack At the Muse (rock n' roll), 44 Surfside Road, ☎ 508-228-6873.

The Moby Dick Bar at The Summer House (piano), 17 Ocean Blvd., Siasconset, ☎ 508-228-9976.

Vincent's (live music throughout the summer months, smoke-free environment), 21 South Water Street, ☎ 508-228-0189.

Reaching Nantucket

There's no need to bring your car to Nantucket. If you're staying in the town of Nantucket, you certainly won't need it, and you can get around the island via the local shuttle service, the **Nantucket Regional Transit Authority**, which operates from 7 a.m.-11:30 p.m. Automobile and bicycle rentals are readily available, too.

By Ferry

From Hyannis, the **Steamship Authority** offers automobile and passenger service (year-round), ☎ 508-477-8600; in Nantucket, ☎ 508-228-0262.

Hy-Line Cruises (passenger only/year-round) offers service between Hyannis and Nantucket. Loacted at the Ocean Street Dock, Hyannis, ☎ 508-778-2600, and at Straight Wharf, Nantucket, ☎ 508-228-3949.

High Speed Catamaran, ☎ 800-492-8082, 508-228-3949, runs to Martha's Vineyard in the summer only and to Straight Wharf, Nantucket.

Freedom Cruise Line (passenger service/seasonal) services Harwich Port and Nantucket. Saquatucket Harbor, Harwich Port, ☎ 508-432-8999; www.capecod.net/freedom.

By Car

To Nantucket (via Hyannis)

From New York City: Follow I-95 to Providence, Rhode Island, then take I-195 to Wareham and Route 25 to the Bourne

Bridge. Pass the bridge and take Route 6 to Route 132, into Hyannis. Follow signs to ferry dock.

From Boston: Follow Route 3 to Route 6, and continue over the Sagamore Bridge to Route 132. Follow signs to ferry dock.

By Air

Cape Air, ☎ 508-771-6944 or 800-352-0714; **Colgan Air**, ☎ 508-325-5100 or 800-272-5488; **Continental Express**, ☎ 800-525-0280; **Island Airlines**, ☎ 508-227-7575, 800-698-1109 (in Massachusetts only), 800-248-7779 (outside Massachusetts); **Nantucket Airlines**, ☎ 508-228-6234 or 800-635-8787; **US Air Express**, ☎ 800-428-4322.

Bus Service (to Hyannis)

Bonanza Bus Line (service to Hyannis from New York and Providence), Hyannis, ☎ 508-775-5524; New York, ☎ 212-947-1766; Providence, ☎ 401-751-8800.

Plymouth and Brockton Bus Line (service between Hyannis and Boston, including Logan Airport), ☎ 508-746-0378.

Amtrak (seasonal service from New York's Penn Station to Hyannis), ☎ 800-872-7245.

Shuttle Service

Nantucket Regional Transit Authority. Children under six and senior citizens over 65 ride free. The downtown shuttle stop are located on Salem and Washington Street.

The following chart shows routes, destinations and fares.

ROUTE	DESTINATIONS	FARE
South Loop	Surfside, Hooper Farm Road and Pleasant Street area.	50¢
Miacomet Loop	Fairgrounds Road, Bartlett Road and Hammock Pond area.	50¢
Madaket Route	Madaket via Cliff Road, New Lane.	$1
'Sconset Route #1	'Sconset via Polpis Road.	$1 o/w
'Sconset Route #2	'Sconset via Old South Road and Nobadeer Farm Road.	$1 o/w

For More Information

Information Bureau, ☎ 508-228-0925.

Nantucket Island Chamber of Commerce, ☎ 508-228-1700

Boston

$\mathcal{I}$'ve included a section on Boston for those of you who might use it as a gateway for your Cape Cod vacation. Even if you're not coming from afar, you should consider spending a day or two in the city before heading to the Cape.

Boston is everything a city should be. It's over three centuries old, and serves as the starting point of our nation's history. The contrast of the old and new is noticeable in the architecture as you stroll around. Follow the Freedom Trail past some of Boston's oldest buildings, such as the Old State House and the Old North Church. Along the same trail you'll find the town's Financial District with tall buildings reaching toward the sky.

Across the Charles River lies Cambridge, home to Harvard University and the Massachusetts Institute of Technology. Harvard Square is eclectic, with street musicians, students, tourists, intellectuals, and a collection of curious onlookers.

The parks of Boston enhance the beauty of the city. Most notable is Frederick Law Olmsted's Emerald Necklace, a string of parks running from downtown through Beacon Hill and Back Bay, along the Charles River and Brookline to Jamaica Pond.

The city is a pedestrian's dream and a driver's nightmare. While many of Boston's sights are within walking distance of one another, many of the streets are one-way for vehicles, which makes reaching the attractions tough. My advice is to walk as much as you can, and take the subway or hail a cab when need be. Boston's subway is run by the MBTA and referred to locals as the "T." It's the nation's oldest mass transit system. It's easy to follow and will be able to get you to many parts of the city.

DONNA M. BLACKBURN

Welcome

Romantic Hotels & Inns

⚹ The Fairmont Copley Plaza Hotel

The Grande Dame of Boston, the Fairmont Copley Plaza is a splendid place to stay. Situated in Boston's prestigious Back Bay neighborhood, the location couldn't be better.

As you enter the hotel, prepare to be stunned by the marble-floored lobby, walls of walnut wood, and mosaic tiles. The ceiling features glass in a paneled screen supported by columns of Italian marble.

Built in 1912 by Clarence Blackall and Henry Hardenbergh, the hotel is an excellent example of Italian Renaissance Revival architecture. Although it has gone through many transformations, much of its original elegance has been retained.

The 379 guest rooms, including 61 elegant suites, are exquisite, with high ceilings and carefully appointed period furnishing reproductions. The guest list here has included members of royal families, U.S. presidents, and Hollywood movie stars.

The hotel has several restaurants, including the opulent Plaza Dining Room, the Copley Restaurant and Bar, and the Tea Court. Amenities include concierge service, 24-hour room service, a full-service executive business center, twice-daily maid service, and nightly turn-down. An on-site health and fitness facility is open from early morning until late evening.

The Fairmont Copley Plaza
138 St. James Avenue
Boston, MA 02116
☎ 617-267-5300; reservations 800-527-4727
Fax 617-247-6681
$$$$

✈ Le Meridien

As a testament to the preservation of older buildings, Le Meridien's transformation from the former Federal Reserve Bank to its current incarnation is of particular note. Built in 1922, the Renaissance Revival granite-and-limestone building was designed by Clipston Sturgis and modeled after a palazzo in Rome.

As part of the renovations, a glass mansard roof was added. The rooms occupying the top three floors feature sloping glass windows with electric drapes. Romantics should ask for a room on one of these floors, overlooking the Norman B. Leventhal Park.

Also romantic are the loft suites on the second floor, each with a handsome sitting room downstairs and an equally attractive loft bedroom nestled upstairs.

The third-floor health club has a pool, Jacuzzi, and large weight room.

The hotel's restaurants are all beautiful. The glamorous and elegant Julien Restaurant has a vaulted gold-leaf ceiling, wingback chairs, and chandeliers. The six-story atrium at the Cafe Fleuri is stunning, offering a blend of light and glamour to the surroundings. Open for breakfast and lunch, The Café also offers its award-winning Saturday Chocolate and Sunday Brunch.

This is a gem of a hotel, located in Boston's downtown. Its European style and elegance can't be beat.

Le Meridien
250 Franklin Street
Boston, MA 02110
☎ 617-451-1900
Fax 617-423-2844
$$$$

The Eliot Hotel

This Back Bay hotel on tree-lined Commonwealth Avenue offers the benefits of old-fashioned luxury at affordable prices.

Most of the guest quarters are suites. The rooms are furnished with understated antique furnishings, English-style chintz fabrics, and Italian marble baths. Modern amenities include in-room fax machines, free movie channels and more. The hotel's restaurant, Clio, serves contemporary French-American cuisine.

The Eliot Hotel
370 Commonwealth
Boston, MA 02215
☎ 617-267-1607
Fax 617-536-9114 or 800-44-ELIOT
$$$$

The Lenox Hotel

Another hotel worth mentioning is the Lenox, also in the Back Bay area. This turn-of-the-century hotel has renovated its 212 rooms to offer deluxe accommodations. The rooms feature warm peach and nutmeg color schemes, rich wood and brass furnishings, velvet upholstery and more; several have working fireplaces. Amenities include 24-hour concierge, personal voice mail, in-room fax machines, laundry service and more. A fitness facility, open from early morning until late evening, is available.

Romantics should inquire about the Romance Packages, which offer chilled champagne and a picnic basket, among other things.

The hotel is now home to the Anago Bistro, located on the first floor, and also features the Samuel Adams Brewhouse, which offers Samuel Adams beers on tap and a light pub menu. Or try the Lenox Upstairs Grille, a recreation of a 16th-century English Pub.

The Lenox Hotel
710 Boylston Street
Boston, MA 02116-2699
☎ 617-536-5300; reservations ☎ 800-471-1422
Fax 617-236-0351
Web site: www.lenoxhotel.com
$$$$

Boston

The Eliot and Pickett Houses

The Eliot and Pickett Houses, in the Beacon Hill district and adjacent to the State Capitol, offer an inexpensive and pleasant bed and breakfast stay. Owned by the Unitarian-Universalist Church, the two houses adjoin one another and include 20 guests rooms with high ceilings, floral wallpaper, and large windows. Many of the rooms have four-poster beds and private baths. A wonderful communal deck overlooks the Boston Commons and State Capitol Building.

Breakfast is a self-service affair. If you'd like to prepare other food items, the kitchen is open to guests.

The houses are popular and advance reservations are recommended. You can't beat the price or location.

The Eliot and Pickett Houses
25 Beacon Street
Boston, MA 02108-2800
☎ 617-248-8707
Fax 617-742-1364
$$

The Newbury Guest House

The location of this guest house is perfect. Situated on very fashionable Newbury Street, it offers an array of pleasant rooms decorated with a simple but subtle Victorian influence. French Impressionist framed prints add a nice touch. A continental breakfast is served in the parlor or on the patio overlooking the street. Rates are very reasonable.

The Newbury Guest House
261 Newbury Street
Boston, MA 02116
☎ 617-437-7666
Fax 617-262-4243
$$

Harborside Inn of Boston

This building was once a mercantile warehouse, built in 1858. The 54 guest rooms are furnished with Victorian-style furniture, queen-size beds, Oriental rugs, and hardwood floors. Several front room suites are particularly spacious. Located in Boston's financial district, the hotel is close to many of Boston's premier attractions. A complimentary buffet continental breakfast is served daily in the café. One of the best deals in Boston.

Harborside Inn
185 State Street
Boston, MA 02109
☎ 617-723-7500
Fax 617-670-2010
$$$-$$$$

The Regal Bostonian Hotel

This first-rate hotel also has a wonderful location and a European flair. Situated across from Faneuil Hall and Quincy Market, visitors staying at the hotel are just minutes away from shops and restaurants. Yet in the confines of your hotel room, you'll feel miles away from the hustle and bustle. The hotel's 152 luxury guest rooms include eight suites. Many guest rooms and suites feature working fireplaces, French doors opening to private balconies, and oversize tubs. The hotel offers guest privileges at a nearby health club. Many amenities are included, such as nightly turn-down service, complimentary newspaper each day, plush robe, umbrella, laundry and valet services and more. The hotel's restaurant, Seasons, has been rated by *Condé Nast Traveler* as one of the top 50 restaurants in the United States.

The Regal Bostonian Hotel at Faneuil Hall Marketplace
Boston, MA 02109-1605
☎ 617-523-3600; reservations, ☎ 800-222-8888
Fax 617-523-2454
http://www.regal-hotel.com/boston
$$$$

Boston

Boston Harbor Hotel

This hotel, located on Rowes Harbor, is quite stunning. The 230-room luxury hotel was part of a $193-million, 15-story Rowes Wharf redevelopment plan. Its arched entrance is remarkable, a defining feature of the waterfront. Most of the guest rooms offers a living room and bedroom combination. The hotel's suites are even more luxurious and several of them come with private terraces. Choose a room with a view of the harbor or the Boston skyline. The hotel's health club and spa offers a full array of weight-training equipment, fitness classes, and a 60-foot heated lap pool. A full range of amenities is available.

The Boston Harbor Hotel
70 Rowes Wharf
Boston, MA 02110
☎ *617-439-7000; direct:* ☎ *617-856-7771*
Fax 617-951-9307
E-mail bhhsales@bhh.com
$$$$

The Marriott Custom House

The Custom House, built in 1847, was once the tallest building in downtown Boston. Marriott has recently renovated the building to its original splendor. Many of the 81 suites which comprise the Custom House are owned by members of the Marriott Vacation International Club, but nightly stays are also available. As you enter the Custom House's Greek Revival Rotunda, you'll marvel at the intricate detail and know you've arrived at a very special place. The guest rooms are handsomely furnished with antique reproductions. On the 25th floor is an observation deck with views of the city. A small museum is also on the premises.

Marriott Custom House
200 State Street
Boston, MA 02109
☎ *617-790-1400*
$$$$

Bed & Breakfast Agency of Boston

One of the best ways to find a romantic place to stay in Boston is to consult a B&B booking agency. The Bed & Breakfast Agency of Boston can book you as a guest in a historical home situated in the waterfront, Faneuil Hall, Back Bay, Beacon Hill or Copley Square neighborhoods.

Bed & Breakfast Agency of Boston
47 Commercial Wharf
Boston, MA 02110
☎ *617-720-3540 or 800-248-9262*
From the U.K., ☎ *0-800-895-128*

Restaurants

Boston

Biba

This sophisticated restaurant is extremely popular for a reason: it has it all. Most important, is the food. Lydia Shire, owner and chef of Biba, has a following spanning several decades and, with co-chef Susan Regis, has created a restaurant well deserving of its reputation. Menu offerings are imaginative. Consider venison chop with shreds of oxtail cooked in a brick oven and served with warm thin pear tart, or Cape scallops dusted in millet with autumn chicory tempura. Other menu choices are equally creative.

The dining room at Biba has a floor inlaid with Brazilian cherry and maple and pale yellow walls complemented by colorful ceiling murals. The restaurant seats 150 people. Romantics should ask for one of the tables overlooking Boston Gardens.

Biba
272 Bolyston Street
Boston, MA 02116
☎ *617-426-7878*
$$$$

Pignoli

Also owned by Lydia Shire, Pignoli offers its guests an equally sophisticated dining experience.

The decor is a remarkable mixture of exotic woods in contrasting shades, free-flowing metal sculptures, and multi-colored marble and terrazzo floors. In summer, an outdoor café is also open. The cuisine is Italian.

Choose from such dishes as crispy red snapper and Tuscan "bean-bean" salad with a spicy red pepper dip, or wild fennel risotto with grilled salmon dolmades and fennel salad.

Adjacent to the restaurant is a wonderful bakery, which sells some of the restaurant's delicious pastries and other fabulous treats.

Pignoli
79 Park Plaza
Boston, MA 02116
Reservations, ☎ 617-338-7500
Fax 617-338-7691
$$$

The Hungry I

Hands down, the Hungry I is the most romantic restaurant in the city. The main dining room is just below street level on Charles Street. As you pass through a narrow alley into the restaurant, you have left the 20th century behind. The main dining room is small, intimate and couldn't be more conducive to romance. The walls are brick, draperies adorn the windows, and antique furnishings decorate the room. On cooler evenings, a fire is set to burn in the fireplace; on warmer nights, the small patio is open for a select few. Upstairs are several additional small dining rooms where many a suitor has orchestrated a wedding proposal. Chef and owner Peter Ballarin specializes in French country cuisine. His prix-fixe menu changes seasonally. Such specialties as swordfish Isabella or rack of lamb with Stilton bordelaise are but a few of the selections offered. The Sunday brunch is also a food-lovers feast.

The Hungry I
71½ Charles Street
Boston, MA 02114
☎ *617-227-3524*
$$$$

Maison Robert

This family-operated French restaurant is a long-standing favorite. Located in the Old City Hall, Maison Robert offers its guests fine French dining in a glamorous and historical setting. The upstairs main dining room is stunning, with a high ceiling, crystal chandeliers, and soft peach walls. Try the roasted rack of lamb with rosemary jus and cream potatoes in puff pastry or braised fillet of salmon with an apple cider saffron sauce. Downstairs is Ben's Café, a smaller restaurant offering equally interesting items: *Sole de la Manche* (sautéed Dover sole with a lobster sauce and sautéed spinach), or fricassee of lobster, corn, tomatoes, potatoes, and chanterelle mushrooms.

Maison Robert
45 School Street
Boston, MA 02108
☎ *617-227-3370*
$$$

The Julien

Imagine vaulted ceilings edged with gold leaf, with five beautiful chandeliers, muted gold and burgundy walls and twinkling candles. This elegant restaurant will set the tone for a romantic evening. Roasted venison filet with chestnuts, fruits and vegetables forestière, or oven-roasted pheasant with Swiss chard pie and wild mushrooms are just two options. Located at Le Meridien Hotel, this is a first-rate, award-winning restaurant. Jacket and tie are required. Reservations recommended.

The Julien
250 Franklin Street
☎ *617-451-1900*
$$$$

Boston

The Union Oyster House

This is the oldest restaurant in Boston, and its charm can't be beat. You'll think you've traveled back in time as you enter the Oyster House and join the guest list that includes John F. Kennedy and Daniel Webster. Fresh seafood is the name of the game here.

The Union Oyster House
41 Union Street
☎ *617-227-2750*
$$$$

Seasons Restaurant at the Bostonian Hotel

Seasons, atop the Bostonian Hotel, is considered one of the Top 50 Restaurants in the United States. It offers the best in romantic dining. Overlooking Faneuil Hall, with piano music quietly playing in the background and the candles glimmering, it's the perfect place to propose or renew your vows. Choose from crêpe annette of lamb with forest mushrooms, sweet potato gnocchi, fava beans, tiny pearl onions, and chianti, or miso-crusted tuna with scallion pancake, baby spinach, and Merlot reduction. After dinner, consider taking a ride in a horse-driven carriage, which line up across the street from the restaurant.

Seasons Restaurant at Faneuil Hall Marketplace
Boston, MA 02109-1605
☎ *617-523-3600*
$$$$

The Hampshire House

This guidebook would not be complete without mentioning the Hampshire House, known for its bar that was featured in the television show *Cheers*. The Bull & Finch Pub has enough *Cheers* memorabilia to satisfy any fans. However, romantics will prefer the sedate beauty of the Library Grille. Here, among an assortment of leather-bound books and paintings, the elegant dining room overlooks the Public Gardens. Entrées include an assortment of New England seafood and contemporary American cuisine, masterminded by head chef Markus Ripperger. Sunday brunch is accompanied by a jazz ensemble.

The Hampshire House
84 Beacon Street
Boston, MA 02108
☎ *617-227-9600*
$$$

DONNA M. BLACKBURN

 *Touring Boston*

Boston's history dates back to 1630, when members of the Massachusetts Bay Company settled here with the promise of religious freedom. By 1632, Boston had been named the capital of Massachusetts. As they say, the rest is history.

The city grew, achieving status as a good place for shipbuilding, fishing, and commerce. The nation's first public school, Boston Latin, opened in 1635; a year later, Harvard was founded.

Then it happened.

Britain began imposing various taxations on the colonies, and America was born as the colonists began to fight back. In 1770, the Boston Massacre occurred at the Old State House. Three years later the famous Boston Tea Party took place as colonists dressed as Indians dumped chests of tea in the Boston Harbor to protest the tax on tea.

It was just a matter of time before a war would begin, and by April 18, 1775, Paul Revere and William Dawes spread the word that the British were about to attack. The next day the "shot that was heard around the world" was fired from Concord and Lexington. Recapture those moments of our nation's history by following the **Freedom Trail**, which takes you past 13 historical sites, including the Old State House, Paul Revere's House and the Old North Church. This 2½-mile trail begins at the Visitor Information Center at the Boston Commons and will take you through downtown Boston, the North End and Charlestown. Your final destination will be the Bunker Hill Monument, built in memory of the men who died in the Battle of Bunker Hill on June 17, 1775.

To walk the Freedom Trail, follow the red line painted on the sidewalk, although it's not always easy to find. Consider taking the 90-minute **National Park Service Tour**, which passes five of the main sites. This informative, well-narrated tour will provide you with a lot of historical information. Call ☎ 617-242-5642 for daily schedules.

Downtown Boston

There's something for everyone in downtown Boston, and with so much to see, you can spend a full day touring the area. At the very heart of the city is **Downtown Crossing**, at the intersection of Summer and Washington streets. Here you will find Macy's, Filene's and Filene's Basement, an assortment of street vendors, bookstores, gift shops and more.

Moments away are several of Boston's most historical sites, including the **Old State House**, at the corner of Washington and State streets. Built in 1713 and restored in 1991-1992, the Old State House was the seat of the original Colonial government. The Declaration of Independence was first read here to the citizens of Boston in 1776. Take note of the building's façade, complete with a large American eagle and a gilded lion and unicorn representing British rule. Housed inside the building is the **Bostonian Society's Museum**, with exhibits featuring three centuries of history. Call ☎ 617-720-3290.

Just outside the Old State House is a ring of cobblestones commemorating the **Boston Massacre**, which took place there on March 5, 1770.

Across the street is **Faneuil Hall**, another historical site where many protest meetings took place before the Revolution. Built in 1742, Faneuil Hall's downstairs is now a lovely marketplace, with many eateries and small shops offering Boston momentos. Next door is **Quincy Market**, a lively shopping center featuring street vendors and an indoor food court. Faneuil Hall is very romantic at night. The trees are draped with twinkling lights and street musicians "play real good for free."

Nearby at Park and Tremont streets is the **Park Street Church**, built in 1809. It was here that the song *America* was first heard on Independence Day in 1832. It was also the place where William Lloyd Garrison gave his first anti-slavery speech, also on Independence Day, in 1829.

To the left is **The Granary Burial Ground**, the resting place for such American heroes as Samuel Adams, John Hancock, and Paul Revere. Also buried here are the five men killed at the Boston Massacre, Benjamin Franklin's parents, and the wife of Isaac Vergoose, also known as "Mother Goose." The burial grounds are open to the public from 8 a.m. until 4 p.m.

Across the street is the **King's Chapel**, built in 1754. Originally an Episcopal Church, it was favored by the British. After the Revolution it became the first Unitarian Church in America. It continues to hold Unitarian-Universalist services. The chapel is open to the public Tuesday through Saturday, from 10 a.m. until 2 p.m. Buried next door are such American notables as William Dawes, who rode with Paul Revere, Mary Clinton, the first woman to step on American soil at Plymouth Rock, and John Winthrop, the first governor of the Massachusetts Bay Colony.

Boston

The magnificent **Massachusetts State House**, where the state does its business, is just down the street. Built by Charles Bullfinch in 1795, its gold leaf dome can been seen for miles.

The Boston Commons was the nation's first park. Originally a cow pasture, it's one of Boston's nicest outdoor spots. Watch the children wade in Frog Pond in the summer, and ice-skate there during the winter months.

Across the street is the **Boston Gardens**, resplendent with flowers throughout the spring and summer months. Take a ride on the famous swan boats here.

The Financial District, Theatre District and China Town are just south of downtown.

The North End

The North End is Boston's oldest neighborhood. The buildings are old, the streets are narrow, and there's never a dull moment here. The North End was originally settled before the Revolution. Since then, it has been the home of a variety of immigrant groups, including the Irish, Eastern European Jews, and Portuguese. In the past century it has been an enclave for Italian-Americans and their influence continues to define this part of the city. On any weekend in the summer, you'll find some sort of festival going on, almost always paying homage to a saint.

The North End is the home of **Old North Church**. It was here that the lanterns were lit from its tall steeple on April 18, 1775, to signal the arrival of the British forces. The church's red-brick façade was built in 1723. The interior of the church has been carefully maintained and has individual pews. Be sure to take a moment to check out pew number 54, once owned by Paul Revere and his family. The church is open daily. Episcopal services are held every Sunday.

Take time to tour **Paul Revere's House**, located at 19 North Square. It was built in 1680 and Paul Revere bought it in 1770. This two-story wooden clapboard house is the oldest standing home in downtown Boston. Open to the public, the interior is filled with 17th- and 18th-century furnishings and artifacts. Call ☎ 617-523-2338 for more information.

Behind the church is the **Paul Revere Mall** (The Prado). This tree-lined park is a good spot to rest your legs before continuing on your tour of the North End.

St. Stephen's Church was designed by Charles Bullfinch in 1804. Restored in 1965, its interior is quite beautiful, featuring chandeliers, white walls, and red carpeting. Catholic services continue to be held here. Located at 401 Hanover. Call ☎ 617-523-1230 for further details.

Boston's historical mid-19th-century maritime past can be re-called at **Lewis Wharf**. Here the clipper-ship trade did much of its business. You can watch locals playing a game of croquet at the Boston Croquet Club, situated to the right of the wharf in the harborside park.

By far the liveliest street in the North End (and that means something because there's never a dull moment anywhere in this area), is **Hanover Street**, where you will find an assort-ment of restaurants and shops. The eateries ranges from cas-ual to elegant, and you're almost certainly be delighted with the food.

Boston

Charlestown

Just a short distance from the North End, Charlestown has its own special flavor. Of much historical significance, Charlestown was settled before Boston, in 1629. Many of the original buildings were destroyed during the infamous Battle of Bunker Hill, which took place in 1775. The **Bunker Hill Monument**, located at Monument Square, commemorates this historical event. You can even climb the 220-foot-tall granite structure, built in 1843. At the base of the monument are several dioramas telling the story of our early nation's most celebrated battle. Park Rangers are also on hand to give more detailed narration. Call ☎ 617-242-5644 for information.

Not to be overlooked are the townhouses surrounding Monument Square. Built in the 1840s, the homes on the square have been nicely preserved.

The *USS Constitution* makes its home at the Charlestown Navy Yard. Nicknamed Old Ironsides, the ship was launched in 1797 and was the chief hero of the War of 1812, winning 42 separate battles. Next door is the **Constitution Museum**, offering further details about the ship's history. Call ☎ 617-426-1812 for more information.

After leaving the Navy Yard, consider taking the MBTA water shuttle to the Long Wharf, a 10-minute ride leaving every half-hour. At a cost of only $1, it's a great way to see the city's harbor and skyline.

The Waterfront

Long Wharf is where Boston's maritime history began more than 300 years ago. The oldest wharf in the city, it was built in 1710. Past the Marriott Long Wharf Hotel is a very nice granite plaza, a good place to sit and look out over the harbor. Here you will also find an embarkment area for an assortment of harbor cruises and tours.

At Central Wharf is Boston's **New England Aquarium**, home of all sorts of sea creatures. The aquarium's special exhibits are often quite interesting. Call ☎ 617-973-5200 for current information. An especially eye-catching feature here is the three-story, 40-foot-diameter tank, with sea turtles, sharks, and an assortment of fish. Next door is the **Discovery Theater**, presenting marine mammal shows throughout the year. More adventurous souls should try a New England Aquarium **Whale Watch Tour**, available throughout the spring and summer seasons. Call ☎ 617-973-5277 for scheduled times and fares.

Spectacular **Rowes Wharf**, in its current incarnation, was built in 1987. Its arched entrance is remarkable and is a prominent feature of the waterfront area. Beyond the arch is the Boston Harbor Hotel and a lovely open space observatory area. Take a stroll on the Harborwalk, past some rather impressive yachts moored here. You will also find a water shuttle service which will take you to Logan Airport.

Down the road apiece is the **Boston Tea Party Ship and Museum**, located at the Congress Street Bridge. The original site of the infamous Tea Party was Griffin's Wharf, but that disappeared long ago. It was in December of 1773 that angry colonists dressed as Mohawk Indians threw 340 chests of tea into the harbor to protest a tax imposed by the British. Re-enact the moment by throwing tea from the side of the ship aboard the *Beaver II*. The tea is roped to the ship, so it's more of a gesture than the real thing, but it's fun anyway. The *Beaver II* is a Danish brig built to resemble one of the three ships which took part in the Tea Party. Call ☎ 617-338-1773 for further details.

Beacon Hill

By far one of the most elegant neighborhoods of Boston, Beacon Hill is just north of downtown. The brownstone and brick buildings are trademarks of the area, as are the brick sidewalks, gas-light street lamps, and tree-lined streets. Of particular note are the brick townhouses lining Mount Vernon Street. Be sure to visit **Louisburg Square**, just down the road apiece, where you will find a small park surrounded by a collection of townhouses. Louisa May Alcott lived at 10 Louisburg Square.

If you'd like to view the interior of a Beacon Hill home, consider a visit to the **Nichols Home Museum**, 55 Mount Vernon Street (☎ 617- 227-6993). The **Harrison Gray Otis House** is also open to the public, at 141 Cambridge Street (☎ 617-227-3956).

Boston

Learn more about African-American history at the **African Meeting House**, 8 Smith Court. The oldest African-American church, it was built by free black artisans in 1806. The **Museum of Afro-American History** is located next door. For an in-depth look at the history of African- Americans in Boston, take the **Black Heritage Trail**. This two-hour tour, conducted by rangers at the National Park Visitor Center, will take you through Beacon Hill and past sites of the Underground Railroad. The tours are held throughout the summer months. Call ☎ 617-742-5415 for more information.

A tour of Beacon Hill is not complete unless you stroll down **Charles Street**. This lovely tree-lined business district has an assortment of romantic restaurants, boutiques and antique shops. It is truly one of the prettiest streets in America.

Charles River Esplanade

The Charles River Esplanade is one of the most romantic places in Boston. Here you can see the Boston skyline on one side of the river, and Cambridge on the other. Sailboats dot the horizon while children play at the river's edge. Skaters, joggers, and bicyclists share the paths on both sides of the river, while others bring picnic lunches or read a book in the afternoon sun. Concerts are held almost every evening at the **Hatch Memorial Shell** (no telephone; check in the *Boston Globe* for latest schedule). The most stunning event of the summer season takes place here. A Boston tradition, the Boston Pops perform a concert preceding the fireworks on the **Fourth of July**.

The annual **Head of the Charles Regatta** brings crews from around the world to compete each fall. Throughout the year, teams of scullers train arduously for the main event.

On Sundays throughout daylight savings time, the stretch of Memorial Drive on the Cambridge side, from Western Avenue Bridge to Eliot Bridge (otherwise known as Riverbend Park) is closed to traffic. The closure allows for a more peaceful stroll near the river's edge.

Located at the Charles River Dam is the **Museum of Science**, offering a vast number of exhibits covering astrophysics, astronomy, natural history and more. The museum also hosts special exhibits, such as the very well received Leonardo DaVinci showing in 1996. Take a break at the museum's Skyline Room Cafeteria. The views of the river from the restaurant are quite splendid.

Next door is the **Mugar Omni Theatre**, which offers 76-foot-wide, four-story-high screen. Become one with the film's shown here as the superb sound system and massive screen brings you right into the picture.

Yoi can reach for the stars at the **Charles Hayden Planetarium**, also housed in the Museum of Science complex.

Call ☎ 617-732-2500 for more information about the museum, the Omni Theatre, and Planetarium.

Back Bay

Back Bay is home to the legendary Brahmins, the Victorian four- and five-story townhouses which define the area. These houses are classy, historical, and truly beautiful.

Back Bay was once considered a wasteland. An industrious movement by land developers included a landfill program that transformed Back Bay to its present state. More orderly than the rest of Boston, the 450 acres which comprise Back Bay run east to west from Beacon Street to Bolyston Street and north to south from Arlington Street to Hereford Street. Old and new collide here, as it does elsewhere in the city. The most stunning example of this juxtaposition is evidenced in **Copley Square**. Here you will find the **Trinity Church**, built in 1877, a French Romanesque-style church, mirrored by the neighboring John Hancock Building, built a century later. Visit the **John Hancock Observatory**, located on the 60th floor of the building, for exquisite views of Boston.

Nearby is the **Copley Place Mall**, one of the prettiest in the United States. Most of the shops are upscale: Neiman Marcus, Tiffany's, and Ralph Lauren have stores here. Next door is the **Prudential Center**, also offering some very nice shops. You can spend a full day in both locations and be perfectly happy. Or travel to the Skywalk, Prudential Center's 50-story observation deck, for a view of the city from above.

Be sure to stroll down **Newbury Street**, just a couple blocks away. This tree-lined avenue offers a delightful mix of very fashionable boutiques and shops. Spend a summer evening here, eating at one of the many restaurants with outdoor seating. As the twinkling lights do their magic, street musicians play Vivaldi and Chopin. This is Boston at its best.

To see Boston as it might have been a hundred years ago, visit **Commonwealth Avenue**, a remarkably beautiful street. The four- and five-story townhouses are shaded by elm trees. Modeled after Paris boulevards, Commonwealth Avenue exudes sophistication and style.

The South End

Boston's South End has been transforming itself of late, and much effort has been made to restore its former elegance. You will find some lovely streets with Victorian row-houses and small community parks. The South End is ethnically diverse and also hosts the largest gay community in Boston. It is an artists' community as well, with many talented folks calling the South End their home.

Tremont and Columbus streets host a number of very nice shops and restaurants, many of which have a subtle European flair about them.

Kenmore Square/Fenway

The Fenway district is comprised of several different areas, each with distinctive characteristics. Here you will find art, baseball, medicine, and education institutions all within a short distance of one another.

The Red Sox have been playing baseball at the famous **Fenway Park** since 1912. **Boston University** and **Northeastern University** are located in the area and just a short distance away is the **Longwood Medical Area**. This vast medical complex includes Harvard Medical School, Children's Hospital, Beth Israel Hospital and Brigham and Women's Hospital.

The **Museum of Fine Arts** is one of Boston's treasures. The works displayed here span centuries and continents. A special emphasis has been placed on 19th-century French art in the Evans Wing, where 38 Monets are part of the museum's permanent collection. Other artists include Millet, van Gogh, Gauguin, Renoir, Picasso, Manet, and Cezanne. The Tenshin-en, Garden of the Heart of Heaven, is a different type of masterpiece. This Japanese garden was designed by Kinsaku Nakane to offer serenity.

The museum sponsors world-class special exhibits and there's always a film festival taking place. It's often necessary to get advance tickets for special exhibits. Call ☎ 617-267-9300 for further details.

The **Isabella Stewart Gardner Museum** is one of my favorite places in Boston and is quite romantic. The museum was home to Isabella Stewart Gardner and her husband, John Lowell Gardner. A native of New York, Ms. Gardner was never quite accepted into Boston's high society. As the saying goes, "Don't get mad, get even." Ms. Gardner built the mansion despite criticism from Boston's society who thought she was over-indulgent. Upon her death, her family turned it into a museum. The mansion was built by Willard T. Sears and was created in the style of an Italian palazzo. Its most stunning feature is the four-story courtyard, where flowers grown in the museum's greenhouse are planted throughout the year. The absolute calm of the courtyard is enough take your breath away... or inspire you to propose or renew your vows. Galleries in the Veronese Room, Gothic Room, Dutch Room, and Titan Room include over 2,000 pieces of art from such notable artists as Botticelli, Rembrandt, Matisse, Sargent, Whistler, and Manet.

Another romantic spot at the museum is the Café at the Gardner, where you can enjoy an excellent lunch on the cafe's outdoor terrace overlooking the museum's gardens.

Throughout the summer, classical concerts are held in the Tapestry Room each weekend. For more information regarding the museum and events taking place there, call ☎ 617-566-1088.

Boston

Cambridge

On the other side of the river lies Cambridge, a city with its on special personality. Its main identity is derived from being the home to Harvard University and the Massachusetts Institute of Technology.

Harvard, our nation's oldest university, is not only the country's leading educational institution, it's also a very attractive campus. Visit Harvard Yard's spacious lawn and gracious trees, surrounded by several original buildings. Students busily walk around with backpacks filled with textbooks and notebooks.

The university houses several museums. My favorites are the **Fogg Art Museum** and the **Botanical Museum**. Take note of The Fogg Art Museum's Italian Renaissance design with a central courtyard. The building houses a nice selection of European art, including works by Rubens, Monet, Renoir, and Picasso. American art is represented by the works of Whistler and Pollock.

The Blaschka Glass Flower collection at the Botanical Museum is exquisite. These hand-blown glass pieces represent 840 plant species and were made by Leopold and Rudolph Blaschka in Germany.

Near Harvard is **Radcliffe College**. Now open to both men and women, this top-notch university was founded in 1879. Visit the Radcliffe Yard, a pretty area surrounded by the college's buildings. The mix of students attending Radcliffe may have changed over the years since it became co-ed, but the yard has maintained much of its original charm.

No visit to Cambridge is complete without a trip to **Harvard Square**. The atmosphere here is absolutely electric. Students, tourists, and street musicians gather here throughout the day and evening. A number of boutiques, art galleries, restaurants, and bookstores complete the scene. There's never a dull moment here.

Exploring Boston

Tours

Trolleys

The following companies offer 90-minute narrated tours and allow you to make a number of stops along the way and reboard at a later time.

The Old Town Trolley Tour of Boston, ☎ 617-269-7010.

Boston Trolley Tours, ☎ 617-TROLLEY.

Red Beantown Trolleys, ☎ 617-236-2148.

The Duck Tours. By land and by sea, Duck Tours offers by far the most imaginative excursions in Boston. Aboard a renovated World War II amphibious vehicle, the guides provide equal parts humor and history to their narration. The boat/bus glides into the Charles River where passengers are asked to steer. It's a blast. ☎ 617-723-DUCK.

Walking Tours

Boston By Foot, 77 N. Washington, ☎ 617-367-2345

Boston Park Rangers, ☎ 617-635-7389

Historic Neighborhoods Foundation, ☎ 617-426-1885

Cruise Tours / Boating Adventures

Boston Harbor Tours offers several historic tours from either Long Wharf, the Navy Yard, or the John F. Kennedy Library. Call ☎ 617-227-4321.

The **Bay State Cruise Company** runs several tours (both of the inner and outer Boston harbors) and also offers whale-watching cruises. ☎ 617-723-7800.

The Spirit of Boston. This is a delightful way to spend a day or evening. Enjoy an authentic New England clambake aboard this 192-foot harbor cruiseship. Serving lunch and dinner. Evening cruises with dancing. ☎ 617-457-1499.

Whale Watching

Whale Watch Safaris. Weekend excursions only. ☎ 617-227-4321.

Boston Harbor Whale Watches. Aboard the *Majestic*, this 4½-hour whale excursion is available daily throughout the season. ☎ 617-345-9866.

Sports

Biking

A great way to see the city is on two wheels. Consult the local telephone directory for bicycle rental shops' phone numbers and locations. Don't try to brave Boston's streets. Your best bet is to stay on the bike paths. Be sure to rent a helmet and lock.

The **Dr. Paul Dudley White Charles River Bike Path** follows the Charles River from the Museum of Science to Watertown. This path offers 17.7 miles of paths.

The Greenbelt Bikeway. This route follows the Emerald Necklace from the Boston Commons in downtown Boston to Franklin Park in Jamaica Pond. This bike path is 8.8 miles long.

Outside of Boston, from the Alewife Station through Arlington, Lexington, and Bedford, the 11-mile **Minuteman Bicycle Path** follows an old railroad track.

Boating/Sailing

Rentals

Community Boating, Inc., 21 Embarkment Road, ☎ 617-523-1038.

Boston Sailing Center, 54 Lewis Wharf, ☎ 617-635-4505.

Charles River Canoe and Kayak Center, 2401 Commonwealth Avenue, Newton, ☎ 617-965-5110.

Annual Events

*T*here are a number of special events in Boston throughout the year. Here is a list of some of the most popular. Consult the *Boston Globe* newspaper or call the Greater Boston Convention and Visitors Bureau (☎ 617-536-4100) for further information.

January

Chinese New Year is celebrated sometime between January 21st and February 19th in keeping with the Chinese calendar. A Dragon Parade, fireworks and more are part of this annual event. The Children's Museum also sponsors Chinese New Year activities.

February

Festivities throughout the month are planned in and around the city as part of the **Boston Festival**. Special events include ice-skating, sledding and ice sculptures.

Several **Valentine's Day** events are scheduled.

March

Celebrated in South Boston, the **St. Patrick's Day Parade** displays Boston's Irish heritage in all its glory.

April

In Massachusetts, **Patriot's Day** takes place on the third Monday of the month. The city celebrates this event by the reenactment of the Battle of Lexington, Paul Revere's and William Dawes' ride and more. Also on this date is the famous **Boston Marathon**.

May

The **Beacon Hill Hidden Garden Tour** takes you to gardens you wouldn't ordinarily have the chance to visit.

The **Boston Pops** begin their season at the Symphony Hall.

June

The **Boston Globe Jazz Festival** is celebrated at the Hatch Shell and other locations throughout the city. In Charlestown, on the weekend closest to June 17th, **Bunker Hill Day** is celebrated. Festivities include a reenactment of an 18th-century military encampment and a parade.

July

The **Annual Boston Harborfest** takes place at the harbor and includes concerts, tours, a chowderfest and more.

On **July Fourth**, the *USS Constitution* leaves the Navy Yard for the Annual Turnaround.

Also on Independence Day, the **Boston Pops Esplanade Orchestra Concert** takes place at the Charles River Esplanade. It's followed by fireworks.

August

The North End celebrates a number of festivals, often in homage to various saints. Food, parades, and children's activities are all part of the fun.

September

The **Boston Film Festival** takes place in a variety of theaters throughout Boston. For film buffs, it's very exciting. Many famous filmmakers, actors, and actresses come to this event.

October

In nearby Salem, the town goes all out to celebrate **Halloween**. Throughout the month Haunted Happenings take place in the town and many of the shops and houses are decorated with witches, ghosts, and goblins.

The **Head of the Charles Regatta** brings crews from around the world to compete in this annual event. It's quite thrilling.

November

The **Nutcracker Suite** opens for the holiday season, at the Wang Center.

December

First Night is celebrated throughout the city on New Year's Eve. Events includes all sorts of activities such as concerts, comedy shows, dance, theater, and more. The ice sculptures in the Boston Commons are particularly beautiful.

Entertainment

Music, dance, and theater are all part of Boston's cultural heritage. The city is home to the Boston Ballet, the Boston Symphony Hall and many other talented groups. Boston's theater district includes the Wang Center for the Performing Arts, the Wilbur Theatre, Colonial Theatre, and the Shubert Theatre, to name a few. Performances vary from classicals and musicals to contemporary theater.

Nightclubs abound in Boston, offering everything from jazz, to classical music to rock n' roll.

Dance

The Boston Ballet. This is the fourth largest dance company in the United States. It offers exquisite classical, contemporary, and avant-garde productions. The Boston Ballet, 9 Clarendon Street, ☎ 617-695-6950 or 617-931-ARTS.

Music

The Boston Symphony Hall was built at the turn of the century. Its Italian Renaissance design is quite stunning. The hall's acoustics are internationally recognized. The Boston Symphony Orchestra plays here from October through April and the Boston Pops calls Symphony Hall their home as well. The Handel and Haydn Society performs regularly, as does an assortment of other international, national, and local groups. Boston Symphony Hall, 301 Massachusetts Avenue, ☎ 617-266-1492.

The **Jordan Hall** at the **New England Conservatory of Music** is a smaller, more intimate hall. Designed in 1903, it sponsors concerts featuring New England conservatory of Music students throughout the year. A variety of chamber music groups perform here as well, including the Juilliard Quartet and the Boston Chamber Music Society. The Jordan Hall at the New England Conservatory of Music, 30 Gainsborough Street (at Huntington Avenue), ☎ 617-262-1120.

Isabella Stewart Gardner Museum. Classical concerts are held in the Tapestry Room every Saturday and Sunday at 1:30 p.m. throughout the summer. Complimentary admission to the museum is included. Isabella Stewart Gardner Museum, 280 The Fenway, ☎ 617-734-1359.

Jazz and folk music are featured in the courtyard at the **Museum of Fine Arts.** Events are held on Wednesday nights during the summer months. Museum of Fine Arts, 465 Huntington Avenue, ☎ 617-267-9300.

Nightclubs/Music

House of Blues (blues), 96 Winthrop, Cambridge, ☎ 617-491-BLUE.

The Regattabar at the Charles Hotel (jazz), 1 Bennett Street, Cambridge, ☎ 617-937-4020.

Johnny D's (eclectic), 17 Holland Street, Davis Square, Somerville, ☎ 617-776-2004.

Theater

The beautiful 1,658-seat **Colonial Theatre** is one of Boston's prizes. Many musical productions have been launched here. A long list of performers who have appeared at the Colonial include such notables as Barbra Streisand, Bob Fosse, and Irving Berlin. The Colonial Theatre, 106 Bolyston, ☎ 617-426-9640.

The **Wang Theatre for the Performing Arts**. This extraordinarily beautiful theatre will take your breath away. Built in the 1920s, the seven-story, 3,800-seat theater is grander than grand. Its Italian marble columns, gold-leaf detailing, mural ceiling, and chandeliers are awesome. So are the performances taking places here, including Broadway musicals, ballet, and opera. The Wang Center for the Performing Arts, 268 Tremont Street, ☎ 617-482-9393.

Another Boston great is the 1910 **Shubert Theatre**, with 1,680 seats. Dramatic giants who have performed here include Sir John Gielgud, Sarah Bernhardt, Ingrid Bergman, and Humphrey Bogart. The Shubert Theatre, 265 Tremont, ☎ 617-426-4520.

Off-Broadway and pre-Broadway productions are the **Wilbur Theatre's** specialties. This 1,200-seat Colonial Revival theater has hosted a number of hits over the years. The Wilbur Theatre, 246 Tremont Street, ☎ 617-423-4008.

Bostix & Ticketmaster

Bostix offers half-price tickets (on the day of the performance) and full-price advance tickets for a variety of Boston's entertainment venues. This cash-only ticket service is located at Faneuil Hall Marketplace and Copley Square. Call ☎ 617-723-5181 for recorded information.

For advance-purchase tickets to a number of Boston's entertainment, sports and other events, call Ticketmaster at ☎ 617-931-2000.

Transportation

In Boston

The Massachusetts Bay Transit Authority (MBTA), offers a great alternative to driving in Boston. The local subway, the "T," will get you almost anywhere you want to go in central Boston. A bus system takes you to places not serviced by the T.

The Commuter Rail allows you to travel to many of the nearby towns and cities in the area. A Visitor Passport can be purchased, allowing you to travel throughout the city for a small fee. The pass can be purchased in advance. Call ☎ 617-722-3200 for more information.

Taxis are available throughout the city. Consult your local telephone directory or take your chances hailing a cab when you need one.

Romantics should consider an evening traveling through Boston in a horse-driven carriage. **Elegant Touch** offers these romantic excursions. Call ☎ 800-497-4350 for details.

Reaching Boston

By Plane

Logan International Airport: The airport is served by all major carriers. Consult a travel agent or individual carriers for fare information.

By Train

Amtrak serves Back Bay and South Station. Call ☎ 800-USA-RAIL for daily departure and arrival times and fare information.

By Bus

The **Bonanza Bus** offers travel to Cape Cod, Rhode Island, Connecticut, and New York. Call ☎ 800-556-3815.

The **Plymouth and Brockton Bus Line** has service from Boston to Cape Cod. Call ☎ 508-746-0378.

Greyhound offers service throughout New England. ☎ 800-231-2222; in Boston, ☎ 617-526-1800.

Boston

For More Information

Greater Boston Convention Center, ☎ 607-536-4100.

Massachusetts Office of Travel & Tourism, ☎ 617-727-3201 or 800-447-6277.

www.city.net/countries/united states/massachusetts/boston.

Index

Index

Index